The Courage to be You

A Guide to Healing & Transformation

Antoinette (Anti) A. Enohmbi

"Healing is not about erasing the past but loosening its grip on your present, so that you can live more freely into your future."

— *Antoinette A. Enohmbi*

Copyright © 2025 Antoinette Okala Enohmbi
The Courage To Be You
December 2025
Published in the U.S.A.
ISBN: 9798994347614

Table of Contents

Dedication

This book is lovingly dedicated to my parents, Alexander Abe Okala (1937-2014) and Mary Ngassa Abe Okala.

The love and memory of my father will always remain dear to my heart. Journeying with him through his final years on earth was a sacred gift— one that revealed my true strength and allowed me to embrace my purpose.

To my mother, Mary Ngassa, I remain profoundly grateful for your unwavering love, support, and guidance. Your steady presence continues to inspire, nurture, and remind me of the power of resilience and grace.

Acknowledgments

This book would not have been possible without the unwavering support of my husband, Dr. Emmanuel Enohmbi, whose belief in my purpose gave me the courage to embark on this journey.

To my brother-in-law, Prince Ojong, thank you for your encouragement and for introducing me to the power of visibility through writing.

To my children, Sean, Marinette, and Emmanuel Junior, your love and patience inspire me to grow every day.

To the seekers group, a group of women, who through prayers and communion, enriched my life and have become a solid support system in my spiritual journey.

I also extend my heartfelt gratitude to Pamela and Charles Anchang for their invaluable advice.

A heartfelt thank-you to my clients, directees, friends, and mentors who have trusted me to walk alongside them on their personal journeys. Your experiences, courage, and transformations continue to fuel my passion for this work.

Finally, to you, the reader, thank you for allowing me to be part of your journey. May this book serve as a guide and a source of inspiration as you embrace the opportunities life presents.

Foreword

Antoinette A. Enohmbi is a rare spiritual guide in a world that often struggles to talk or write about grief and spirituality. In this book, she combines a practical, forward-focused approach to life coaching with a deep, reflective thought process designed to help individuals and families from various sociopolitical, economic, cultural, and racial backgrounds rewrite their stories, reclaim their identities, and apply intellectual, psychological, spiritual, and emotional intelligence to live what she aptly calls their "best life."

At the book's opening, Antoinette states, "Healing is not about erasing the past but loosening its grip on your present, so that you can live more freely into your future." This unique blend offers a path forward that honors both the human heart and the soul.

Clinicians and psychiatrists are reporting an increase in mental illnesses among young people, conditions that contribute to the global burden of disease and disability. Widespread misinformation and disinformation, along with

1

a comorbidity of profuse use of social media, are causing devastating psychological and emotional problems. These include depression, increased anxiety, negative self-image, feelings of loneliness, fear of being ignored, cyberbullying, and financial losses through widespread scamming. Widespread military and socio-economic conflicts leading to the displacement of large populations have created societal pressures that add to the erosion of core values of humanity.

We need to take a new direction, a reset of our values, actions, and beliefs. This is not just about educating ourselves and fully understanding our shortcomings, but also about taking steps to recognize our abilities and reclaim our power. Investing in or balancing our physical efforts and techniques acquired through structured and experiential learning with the supranatural — self-belief properties — can get us there.

This book strives to fill that gap. It is a masterclass in holding space. It is a compassionate companion that will walk with you through the "tear in the Universe" that comes with loss, helping you find meaning and peace. It is, in a way, a safe space for the grieving person to talk, process, and navigate the complexities of grief at their own pace. The book does not attempt to fix or rush the process; instead, it provides a gentle map for the journey ahead. In this book, the author seeks to serve people struggling with grief, addiction, or facing significant life changes. It offers options for individuals seeking clarity, transformation, and support in pursuing their goals and living a more fulfilling life. It provides spiritual guidance for those seeking a deeper connection with God or their spiritual journey.

With this, the author and coach offer a powerful invitation to move through grief with intention and spiritual awareness. I urge you to accept that invitation, open these pages, and begin the sacred work of healing. Antoinette Enohmbi reminds us that it is a journey of healing and growth, and a purpose worth pursuing. In her own words, "Coaching offers us the opportunity to enjoy life in full."

I have had the privilege of knowing Antoinette for more than ten years. I have witnessed her deep compassion for people, her caring nature, her spiritual direction, her role as a friend, mother, and wife, her faith in God, holy matrimony, and her efforts in helping the community grow. Antoinette has extraordinary skill in helping people navigate loss and manage psychophysical pain not by offering platitudes but by creating space for profound transformation, as we glean from the testimonies of her clients.

I am confident that you will benefit from reading this book and getting more information at www.tlifecoachinggrief.com. You will find soul-centered conversations rooted in deep, holy listening and discernment, among other things.

Prof. Dr. Emanuel K. Ngwainmbi

Chapter 1: Meet Antoinette (Anti) A. Enohmbi

"Your story is the foundation of your strength, and your healing can become the bridge for others."

Antoinette A. Enohmbi

For many years, I resisted the idea of writing despite my husband's persistent encouragement. Having witnessed the depth of my gift and purpose, he believed I should share my talent with the world.

As my life and grief coaching and spiritual direction practice (tlifecoachinggrief.com) grew, and I sought to expand my virtual presence, my brother-in-law, Prince Ojong—a business architect and marketing expert— echoed this encouragement. He introduced me to the book *Celebritize Yourself: The Three-Step Method to Increase Your Visibility and Explode Your Business*, which opened my eyes to the power of storytelling and personal branding. Gradually, I became intrigued by the idea of sharing my experiences, knowledge, and

1

expertise—or my gift, as my husband calls it—to inspire and empower others. As a trained and certified life coach, grief coach, and spiritual director/companion, I have had the privilege of journeying with clients as they transform life's challenges into meaningful opportunities and dream-of solutions. With a deep passion for listening and engaging in thought-provoking conversations, I have witness the profound power of self-discovery and personal growth.

My Journey into Coaching

When people meet me today, they often see the titles first: Certified Life & Grief Coach, Certified Spiritual Director and Companion, entrepreneur, public speaker, A child of God, daughter, wife, mother, sister, and friend. These titles are part of who I am, but they are not the whole of me. They are milestones, not the essence. Beneath each certification and every role lies a story—one woven with threads of joy and pain, loss and renewal, fear and courage.

My story begins in Buea, Cameroon, where I was born as the fifth of eight children. Our family moved frequently because of my father's job. Each new city meant saying goodbye to familiar friends and surroundings and starting over again. For a quiet, shy, and rule-following child like me, these transitions were often overwhelming. I did not always have the courage to speak my mind or stand out. Instead, I learned to listen—closely, intently, with a kind of attentiveness that would later become one of my greatest gifts as a coach.

I grew up in a culture where children were expected to be seen, not heard. Expressing your feelings too openly could be misinterpreted as disrespect. I learned to hold my emotions inside, often suppressing them for fear of being misunderstood, and yet in the silence of my heart, I found another gift awakening—the gift of **discernment and presence.** Friends and family would share their joys and sorrows with me, sensing that I was a safe place. Listening without judgment became my way of caring for others long before I had the language of "coaching" or "spiritual direction." Looking back, it was God working within me, shaping me for something I could not yet see. What I thought was shyness was, in fact, preparation. God was teaching me to listen deeply, to hold silence, and to notice the quiet whispers of both human hearts and the Holy Spirit.

The Gift of Education

Education became one of the strongest pillars of my transformation. My father believed in the power of education—not only for his children but also for others who crossed his path. He quietly paid the tuition of students who were not even related to us, some of whom came forward only at his funeral to share how his generosity changed their lives. Watching his example impressed upon me the value of lifting others up through knowledge, opportunities, and compassion.

I carried that belief with me when I arrived in the United States after high school. Leaving Cameroon was both exhilarating and intimidating. I was stepping into a world that was unfamiliar, where cultural differences challenged me to adapt quickly. Attending Montgomery College in Maryland gave me a

4

foundation, but it was at Bowie State University, where I earned my Bachelor of Arts in Psychology, that I truly began to understand the complexity of the human mind and the importance of self-discovery.

My spiritual hunger led me to Fairfield University in Connecticut, where I completed a four-year formation program in Spiritual Direction. This was not just an academic pursuit but a transformative journey of its own. Through prayer, reflection, and guidance, I discovered a God who was not distant or judgmental, but near, compassionate, and desiring a personal relationship with me. This discovery radically shifted the way I viewed myself and others.

Later, I pursued a Certificate in Professional Life Coaching (CPLC) at the University of North Carolina, Charlotte, in collaboration with the International Association of Professional Recovery Coaches (IAPRC), a program accredited by the International Coaching Federation (ICF). This rigorous training taught me the structure, ethics, and discipline of professional coaching, while also validating the natural gifts I had been cultivating for years.

To serve those who were struggling with grief and major changes in life, I also earned certification with the Institute of Professional Grief Coaching (IOPGC). A program accredited by the International Coaching Federation (ICF). This training equipped me with tools and resources to help people process their emotions, establish healthy coping mechanisms, and rebuild their lives after a loss in meaningful ways.

Each qualification added another layer to my growth, but more importantly, it expanded my ability to walk alongside others with authenticity, compassion, and wisdom.

Living Between Roles: Motherhood, Marriage, and Calling
Life coaching isn't something I just learned in a classroom; it is something I lived. My journey in the United States was full of change, transitions, and challenges. After graduating from college, I got married and started a family. I later moved with my family from Maryland to New York, where I worked with the New York school system as a Special

Education teacher, and eventually to North Carolina. Each move meant rebuilding community, starting anew, and finding my footing all over again.

When I became a mother to three children under the age of four, my days became a blur of childcare activities, school runs, and after-school activities, while managing the household, and supporting my husband's demanding career. There were moments when I wondered if I was enough — enough of a mother, enough of a wife, enough of a professional. The internal dialogue was constant, sometimes harsh, and often discouraging.

Yet, amid it all, I leaned on my faith. Prayer became my anchor. Scripture became my compass. I remembered the words from Isaiah 41:10: *"So do not fear, for I am with you; do not be dismayed, for I am your God. I will strengthen you and help you; I will uphold you with my righteous right hand.* These words reminded me that I was not walking this path alone.

Balancing all my roles was never about perfection; it was about presence. I learned that even in chaos, I could pause, breathe, and choose love. That choice, repeated, helped me grow stronger and more confident.

The Heart Behind My Coaching
What makes my approach to coaching unique is that it is rooted in both lived experience and spiritual wisdom. I know what it feels like to lose a loved one and still have to wake up and show up for life. I know what it feels like to be an immigrant navigating cultural differences while longing for belonging. I know the struggle of balancing motherhood, marriage, work, and personal dreams without losing yourself in the process.

These experiences taught me that people don't need someone to "fix" them. What we truly need is someone who can listen deeply, ask powerful questions, and hold a safe space for us to discover our own inner resources. As a **Life Coach**, I guide individuals through transitions, helping them align their daily choices with their deeper values. As a **Grief Coach**, I accompany those who are carrying heavy losses, gently walking with them as they move from heartbreak toward healing, and from grief to gratitude. And as a **Spiritual Director**, I create sacred spaces for people to encounter God in their everyday lives, to hear His whisper in both their joys and struggles.

At the core of my philosophy is what I call the mirror principle: if you want to change your life, you must first be willing to look inward. Just as a mirror reflects our outward appearance, our inner world reflects what we believe about ourselves. If we see ourselves through the lens of guilt, fear, or unworthiness, we will live small. But if we dare to see ourselves through God's eyes—beloved, capable, and resilient—we open the door to transformation.

The Power of Story in Transformation

Stories have always been central to my journey. As a child, I lived through experiences that shaped my understanding of life, even when I couldn't name them. Later, I encountered books and mentors whose stories lit a path forward for me. One of the most transformative books I read during my formation program was *A Friendship Like No Other* by William Barry. In it, I discovered that prayer is not about reciting the right words or presenting myself as flawless before God. Instead, prayer is a **relationship**, an honest conversation with a friend who knows me fully and loves me unconditionally. This shifted everything, and I realized I could talk to God the way I would talk to a dear friend—sharing my joys, my disappointments, my anger, and my gratitude. That practice has not only deepened my spiritual life but has also shaped the way I walk with my clients. I encourage them to tell their stories honestly, to bring both their pain and their dreams into the light, and to trust that they are not alone in the journey.

I once told my father that I wanted to emulate his forgiving and gentle spirit, and I now invite others to see themselves as capable of growth, healing, and reinvention. My father's legacy of generosity and compassion continues to whisper to me, *"Lead with love, and the rest will follow."*

Reflection Prompts
Take time to reflect on the following questions in your journal:

- ◆ What personal experiences have shaped the way you listen to others?

- ◆ How has your family background, culture, or upbringing influenced your view of yourself?

- ◆ When you look in the mirror, what do you see? What do you wish to see?

- ◆ Which parts of your story do you feel called to share with others?

- ◆ How might your life experiences be preparing you to guide, mentor, or inspire someone else?

Closing Invitation

My journey has been full of transitions—across countries, roles, and life seasons. Through it all, I have discovered that God wastes nothing. Every joy, every disappointment, every challenge has become part of the tapestry of who I am today.

As you reflect on your own life story, I encourage you to pause and see the threads that your life journey has been weaving. What gifts have you been cultivating? What lessons have you learned in silence, in sorrow, and in joy?

Remember this: your story matters. Not only does it matter for your own growth, but it may one day become the very light someone else needs in their darkness.

Let's walk together on this journey. I am here to listen, to support, and to help you discover the masterpiece that you are

Chapter 2: Introduction to Transformative Life Coaching

"Each of us carries within a hidden masterpiece, waiting to be revealed. Coaching is the brush that helps us paint it into being."
                              -Antoinette A. Enohmbi

The Making of a Life, Grief Coach & Spiritual Director

When I look back on my life, I can clearly see the threads that led me to become a Certified Life Coach and Spiritual Companion. Since childhood, I have been more of a listener than a talker. I found comfort in being present for others, hearing their stories, and holding their pain even when I struggled to make sense of my own. My early years in Cameroon taught me the importance of community, respect, and faith—but they also shaped in me a deep awareness of how easy it is to feel unseen, unheard, or misunderstood.

As a young girl, I often doubted my own abilities. I worked hard in school, but I rarely felt "good enough." My quiet nature meant that I stayed in the background, absorbing the emotions and stories around me, and that gift of listening would later become one of the most powerful tools in my work as a coach. I know what it feels like to long for someone to truly hear you, not to fix you, but to witness you.

When I moved to the United States after high school, I found myself in a culture where self-expression was celebrated. It was a dramatic shift from the environment I grew up in, where silence and obedience were often valued more than voice and individuality. This transition cracked something open in me. I realized that I had a deep longing to embrace my authentic self, to redefine what success meant, and to support others to do the same.

My journey through caregiving, loss, and personal transformation eventually led me to pursue training in Life and Grief Coaching and in Spiritual Direction. While these are distinct practices, both share a common thread: they create safe, compassionate spaces where people can explore their stories, discover their inner strengths, and uncover new possibilities for their lives.

This book is my offering to you. It is both a reflection of my own journey and a practical guide that empowers you to begin your own. Think of it as a gentle companion—part

mirror, part map, and part encouragement—
helping you step into the person you are called
to be.

The Heart of Transformative Life Coaching
At its core, transformative life coaching is not
about fixing you. You are not broken. Instead,
it is about unlocking the wisdom, resilience,
and creativity that already live inside you.
Coaching helps you to:

- Clarify your goals and values.
- Recognize limiting beliefs and gently
  challenge them.
- Reframe obstacles as opportunities for
  growth.
- Take purposeful, aligned action that
  reflects your true self.

Unlike traditional coaching, which often
focuses solely on external goals or
performance, transformative coaching goes
deeper. It looks at the beliefs, patterns, and
stories that shape your choices. It helps you
align your inner life with your outer actions so
that success is not just measured in

achievements, but also in fulfillment, peace, and meaning.

I often tell my clients, *"Life coaching is like using a search engine. The answers are already there—the key is knowing which questions to ask."* Through this process, you become both the seeker and the finder. You gain the tools to ask the right questions, uncover hidden truths, and step into a life that feels authentically yours.

Key Principles of Transformative Coaching
Transformative coaching is not about quick fixes or surface-level changes. It is about shifting the very foundations of how you see yourself, how you respond to life, and how you move forward with purpose. At its heart are five guiding principles—pillars that create a path toward clarity, healing, and growth.

These principles are not abstract theories. They are lived experiences, cultivated through awareness, action, and reflection. Whether you are seeking personal healing, professional growth, or deeper spiritual alignment, these principles can serve as your compass for lasting transformation.

1. Self-Awareness as the First Step

Every journey of change begins with awareness. Transformation starts the moment you pause and notice your thoughts, emotions, and behaviors without judgment.

Most of us live on autopilot, repeating the same habits, telling ourselves the same stories, and reacting to life in familiar ways. Coaching invites you to step off autopilot and become a mindful observer of your inner world. You begin to ask:

- *What thoughts are shaping my choices?*

- *Which emotions rise most often—and what are they teaching me?*

- *What patterns keep repeating in my life, and why?*

With awareness comes freedom. Instead of being trapped by old reactions, you gain the ability to choose a different response. You realize that you are not defined by your past, your fears, or even your mistakes. You are defined by the choices you make now.

Practical tools for cultivating self-awareness include journaling, mindfulness practices, and coaching conversations that mirror back your strengths, blind spots, and untapped potential.

Awareness is the doorway. Once opened, it reveals the power to reshape your life.

Reflection Questions

- Where in your life are you operating on autopilot?

- What thoughts or stories come up most often when you face challenges?

- Practice Exercise: Keep a "self-awareness journal" for one week. Each day, write down one recurring thought or emotion you notice. Ask yourself: *What does this reveal about me? Do I want to keep this pattern, or shift it?*

2. Healing and Release

Transformation is not about erasing the past— it is about loosening its grip on your present. Many of us carry unhealed wounds: the pain of rejection, disappointment, or internalized beliefs whispering that we are not enough.

These stories become invisible anchors, holding us back from stepping into our fullest selves.

In coaching, healing begins with naming what has been hidden. When clients articulate their pain in a safe, nonjudgmental space, the burden begins to lift. The process of speaking truth—of saying "This hurt me" or "This shaped me"—creates the possibility of release.

Healing does not mean forgetting. It means reclaiming your power so that the past no longer dictates your future. Through tools such as reframing, forgiveness practices, and self-compassion exercises, coaching helps clients see their wounds not as life sentences but as teachers.

The release creates space for something new, new energy, new possibilities, new hope.

Reflection Questions

- What old stories or beliefs are you still carrying?

- How do these wounds show up in your present choices?

Practice Exercise

19

Write a letter (you don't have to send it) to a past version of yourself who went through pain. Acknowledge their hurt, thank them for surviving, and gently release the story they carried.

3. Living by Core Values

When your actions align with your deepest values, life begins to flow. Decisions feel clearer, energy feels lighter, and confidence grows. Conversely, when your daily choices conflict with your values, stress, resentment, and confusion take root.

One of the most powerful gifts of coaching is supporting clients to uncover what truly matters. Sometimes, we inherit values from family or culture without asking if they still serve us. Other times, our values are buried under years of obligation or busyness.

Through reflection, clients often rediscover their core truths:

- For some, it is family and love.

- For others, it is creativity, service, or faith.

- For many, it is growth and authenticity.

Living by your values is not about perfection; it is about direction. Every decision becomes an opportunity to ask: *Does this align with who I want to be?*

When alignment happens, clients experience a new sense of ease. Life may still be challenging, but it no longer feels fragmented. The inner compass is clear, and every step builds integrity and wholeness.

Reflection Questions

- What values matter to you?

- Where in your life are you living in alignment with them—and where are you not?

Practice Exercise

List your top five values. Then look at your past week and identify one moment where your actions reflected those values, and one moment where they didn't. Consider how you can shift future decisions toward alignment.

4. Empowered Action

Insight without action is like a seed never planted—it holds potential but never bears fruit. In transformative coaching, breakthroughs in awareness are only the beginning. True transformation requires movement.

Empowered action means translating your clarity and values into aligned choices. These actions are not rooted in fear or obligation but in authenticity and purpose. Instead of striving to prove yourself or please others, you act because the step feels true to who you are becoming.

The Anatomy of Empowered Action:

1. Clarity: Knowing what matters and why.

2. Alignment: Ensuring actions reflect your values and goals.

3. Accountability: Creating systems to stay committed.

Practical tools include chunking big goals into small steps, using "if–then" planning (e.g., *If it's 7 a.m. on Monday, then I walk for 30 minutes*), and celebrating small wins to build momentum.

Transformation becomes a lifestyle when empowered action is consistent. Each choice, however small, reinforces courage and builds confidence. Over time, the client realizes: *I am no longer waiting for change. I am living it.*

Reflection Questions

- What is one action you've been avoiding, even though you know it matters?

- What would change if you took one small step today?

Practice Exercise

Choose one goal. Break it into three small actions you can take this week. Write them down with deadlines. At the end of the week, review: Did I follow through? What did I learn?

5. Resilience and Growth

No matter how aligned or empowered we are, life will bring setbacks. Transformation is not about avoiding difficulty; it is about rising through it. This is where resilience becomes essential.

Resilience is not stoic toughness. It is the ability to bend without breaking, to adapt without losing hope. It is graceful to feel your emotions deeply while still choosing to move forward.

In coaching, resilience is cultivated through reframing challenges, practicing self-compassion, and identifying support systems. Clients learn to see obstacles not as evidence of failure but as stepping stones for growth.

A decisive shift occurs when clients begin asking not, *"Why is this happening to me?"* but *"What is this teaching me?"*

Research confirms what many of us know from experience that adversity can be the soil of transformation. People who rise from challenges often emerge with deeper gratitude, stronger relationships, and a clearer sense of purpose. This is known as post-traumatic growth.

Resilience is not only for yourself; it also becomes a legacy. When you model resilience, your children, colleagues, or community—are inspired to rise as well.

Reflection Questions

- What past challenge shaped you into who you are today?

- How can you use your current struggles as lessons rather than limitations?

Practice Exercise

Think of a recent setback. Write down three lessons it taught you and one way it made you stronger. Keep this list somewhere visible as a reminder of your resilience.

Conclusion: The Transformative Cycle

Transformation is not a straight path. It is a cycle:

Awareness → Healing → Alignment with Values → Empowered Action → Resilience and Growth.

Each stage feeds into the next. Awareness reveals wounds. Healing clears the way. Values give direction. Action creates movement. Resilience sustains growth.

When people embrace these principles, they discover that transformation is not about becoming someone else. It is about becoming more fully themselves—clearer, freer, more purposeful, and more alive.

From Self-Discovery to Community Impact
One of the most beautiful aspects of transformative life coaching is that its effects rarely stop with the individual. When you grow, you inspire others. When you learn to listen deeply to yourself, you naturally begin to listen more compassionately to others. When you step into your purpose, you give others permission to do the same.

I have witnessed this ripple effect countless times. A client who once struggled with self-doubt became more confident in her career, and soon her colleagues were inspired by her courage to speak up. Another client who learned to process grief with compassion began volunteering to support others in similar situations. Transformation spreads because authentic growth is contagious.

This book is not only about coaching yourself; it is about becoming a source of light in your community. As you practice these principles and tools, you will find yourself better equipped to encourage, uplift, and guide those around you. You may even discover a calling to companion others more intentionally, whether as a coach, mentor, or simply as a compassionate presence.

Reflection Prompts

- What beliefs about yourself have you carried since childhood that may no longer serve you?

- When have you felt truly seen and heard, and how did it affect your sense of self?

- Which areas of your life feel most aligned with your values right now? Which feels out of alignment?

- If your life were a painting, what colors, images, or symbols would it include? What would you like to add to that picture moving forward?

Closing Thoughts

Transformative life coaching is both a process and a relationship. It is a journey of self-discovery, healing, growth, and partnership that empowers you to step into your best and most authentic self. This is not about becoming someone else; it is about uncovering the masterpiece that has always been within you.

As you move through the pages of this book, I invite you to pause, reflect, and practice. Take the tools that resonate with you, try the exercises, and listen for the whispers of your own inner wisdom. You are both the artist and the canvas. And I am here to walk alongside you, to encourage you, and to remind you that you have everything you need to create a life of balance, fulfillment, and joy.

Reflection Question: What masterpiece is waiting within you, and what first brushstroke are you ready to take today?

Chapter 3: Methods and Tools for Transformation

"Every practice, no matter how small, can become a seed of change. With the right tools, those seeds blossom into growth, gratitude, and purpose."

— *Antoinette A. Enohmbi*

While the heart of coaching lies in presence, listening, and meaningful conversation, practical tools can deepen the process. Here are some of the most impactful methods I use in my coaching practice:

1. Neuro-Linguistic Programming (NLP)

Neuro-Linguistic Programming, often called NLP, is based on the idea that our thoughts, language, and behaviors are interconnected. The way we speak to ourselves—both consciously and subconsciously—shapes our reality.

For example, a client who constantly repeats the thought *"I'm not good enough"* may subconsciously create patterns of self-sabotage or avoidance. NLP techniques such as reframing (looking at a situation from a new perspective) or anchoring (associating positive emotions with specific triggers) help clients interrupt these old patterns and create new, empowering ones.

Through NLP, clients begin to:

- Recognize the "scripts" they have been living by.

- Challenge negative self-talk that keeps them stuck.

- Rewrite their internal narrative into one that supports growth and resilience.

Someone I know transformed their career confidence through NLP. She had long believed she wasn't "leadership material." By working together to reframe her limiting beliefs and anchor moments of past success, she began walking into meetings with a new mindset: *"I have a voice worth hearing."* That subtle shift opened doors to new opportunities.

At its core, NLP equips people with the tools to notice when old stories surface and consciously replace them with beliefs that nurture growth, clarity, and courage.

Reflection Questions:

- What limiting beliefs or self-talk phrases do you find yourself repeating most often?

- Where do you think those beliefs came from (family, culture, past experiences)?

- How would your life change if you replaced those beliefs with empowering ones?

2. Visualization and Mental Rehearsal

The human mind cannot always distinguish between vividly imagined experiences and real ones. This is why athletes, public speakers, and leaders often use visualization and mental rehearsal to achieve peak performance.

Visualization is more than daydreaming—it is a structured practice of creating a mental picture of your desired outcome. For example:

- An individual preparing for a job interview might visualize walking into the room with calm confidence, shaking hands firmly, and answering questions with clarity.

- A client working on fitness goals may imagine crossing the finish line of a 5K, feeling strong and accomplished.

These exercises engage the same parts of the brain as real-life action, making the envisioned outcomes feel more attainable and motivating.

In coaching, I often guide clients through "future self" visualizations—a journey where they meet their best possible selves five or ten years from now. This "best self" isn't fantasy; it's a mirror of the person they can become when they align choices with values. Clients often walk away with renewed energy, clarity, and a belief that change is possible.

Visualization transforms vague hope into felt experience, motivating clients to take real, consistent steps toward making their vision a reality.

Reflection Questions:
- If you could meet your "future self" 5 years from now, what would you want to see?

- What does success look and feel like in the area of your life you most want to change?

- What small step could you take today that would move you closer to that vision?

3. The Wheel of Life

The Wheel of Life is one of the simplest yet most profound tools in coaching. It gives clients a snapshot of their overall life balance across key areas such as:

- Career & Work
- Relationships & Family
- Health & Wellness
- Spirituality & Faith
- Finances
- Personal Growth
- Fun & Recreation
- Contribution & Service

Clients rate their satisfaction in each area, usually on a scale of 1–10. When these ratings are plotted on a circular "wheel," the gaps and imbalances become clear. For example, a client might score high in career and finance but low in relationships and health. The wheel is then "flat," showing that although some areas are thriving, others need attention to create a smoother, more fulfilling life journey.

The beauty of the Wheel of Life is its simplicity. In just one exercise, clients gain perspective on:

- Where their energy is currently flowing.

- Which areas feel neglected or draining.

- Where small shifts could create greater harmony.

One client realized through this tool that although she was thriving professionally, she had scored herself a "2" in self-care. That wake-up call prompted her to create new rhythms for rest and joy—leading to more balance overall.

The Wheel of Life reminds us that transformation is not about excelling in just one area but about nurturing the whole self.

Reflection Questions:
- Which areas of your life feel most satisfying right now?

- Which areas feel neglected or draining?

- If your life were a wheel, would it roll smoothly—or would it feel bumpy and uneven?

4. The GROW Model

The GROW Model is one of the most effective and widely used frameworks in coaching. It stands for Goal, Reality, Options, and Will. This structured process helps individuals clarify what they want to achieve, assess their current situation, explore possible pathways, and commit to concrete actions. Its strength lies in its simplicity—making even the biggest goals feel attainable while keeping clients accountable and focused.

Why the GROW Model Works

- It transforms vague desires into clear, measurable goals.

- It encourages honest self-reflection about where you currently stand.

- It opens creative thinking by exploring multiple possibilities.

- It ends with firm commitment, ensuring progress through action.

Applying the GROW Model Step by Step

1. Goal – Define What You Want

- Identify a specific, meaningful goal you want to achieve.

- Make it measurable and time-bound.
- *Example:* "I want to lose 10 pounds in the next three months."

2. Reality – Assess Where You Are Now

- Reflect honestly on your current situation.
- Ask yourself questions such as:
    - What is my current weight?
    - How often do I exercise now?
    - What are my eating habits like?
- This step creates awareness and reveals what is holding you back.

3. Options – Explore the Possibilities

- Brainstorm all potential ways to move forward. Don't censor your ideas at this stage.
- *Examples for weight loss:*
    - Begin a regular workout routine three times per week.
    - Reduce processed foods and focus on whole, nutrient-rich meals.
    - Cut back on food portions.

- Hire a personal trainer or join a fitness class for accountability.

- Once you've listed the options, evaluate which are most realistic and motivating for you.

4. Will – Commit to Action

- Decide what specific steps you will take and when.

- Create accountability by setting deadlines.

- *Example:* "I will work out for 30 minutes on Monday, Wednesday, and Friday, and I will track my meals in a food journal daily."

- Ask yourself: *What obstacles might arise, and how will I overcome them?*

By walking through these four stages, you move from a broad intention to a detailed, practical plan. The GROW Model creates a clear roadmap for success, breaking the journey into manageable steps while ensuring accountability and motivation.

Coaching Insight: As simple as this model is, it can be applied to any area of life—career growth, relationships, financial goals, health, or personal development. Wherever you feel stuck, GROW can help you move forward with clarity, confidence, and purpose.

5. **SMART Goals**

One of the most powerful tools in coaching is the SMART framework for goal setting. SMART ensures your goals are clear, structured, and achievable. Vague intentions like *"I want to do better at work"* often lead to frustration and inaction. SMART goals transform those intentions into a roadmap for success by making them Specific, Measurable, Achievable, Relevant, and Time-bound.

Step-by-Step Breakdown

1. Specific

   o Goals should be clear and precise, leaving no room for ambiguity.

   o Ask: *What exactly do I want to accomplish? Why is this important? Who is involved?*

   o *Example:* Instead of "I want to be healthier," say, "I want to run a 5K without stopping."

2. Measurable

- o Progress must be trackable, with clear criteria for success.

- o Ask: *How will I know I'm making progress? What will success look like?*

- o *Example:* "I will track my running distance and time each week until I can complete 3.1 miles."

3. Achievable

- o The goal should be realistic based on your resources, skills, and circumstances.

- o Ask: *Is this within my reach? What do I need to succeed?*

- o *Example:* If you've never run before, starting with a 5K in six months is achievable; aiming for a marathon in the same timeframe may not be.

4. Relevant

- o Goals should align with your values, priorities, and long-term vision.

- Ask: *Does this matter to me right now? How does it support my bigger picture?*
- *Example:* If improving health will boost your energy for family and work, it's clearly relevant.

5. Time-bound

- Every goal needs a deadline to create urgency and accountability.
- Ask: *When will I achieve this?*
- *Example:* "I will run a 5K by July 15th."

Example: Career Promotion

- Specific: "I want to be promoted to Senior Project Manager."

- Measurable: "I'll take on two extra projects per quarter and track performance reviews."

- Achievable: "I already meet the technical requirements; I need to sharpen my leadership skills."

- Relevant: "This promotion will advance my career, increase my salary, and allow me to mentor others."

- Time-bound: "I will achieve this within the next 6 months."

The power of SMART goals lies in their clarity. When clients shift from vague intentions to structured goals, they feel motivated and confident. SMART goals turn the abstract into the actionable, reminding us that transformation is less about wishing and more about creating a realistic path forward.

Key Takeaway: *Big dreams become achievable when broken into SMART steps.*

6. Mindset + Action = Results

Transformation doesn't come from wishful thinking—it is the direct outcome of aligning what you *believe* with what you *do*. This simple yet powerful equation—Mindset + Action = Results—reminds us that success is born when our thoughts and beliefs fuel consistent, purposeful action.

Even the most detailed plan will fail without the right mindset. And even the most positive mindset will not produce change without action. True results require both.

The Role of Mindset

Mindset is the internal foundation of transformation. It influences how you interpret challenges, setbacks, and opportunities.

- A fixed mindset says: "I can't do this; I'll never be good enough."

- A growth mindset says: "I may not know this yet, but I can learn, adapt, and improve."

Coaches help clients shift toward a growth mindset by challenging limiting beliefs, reframing negative self-talk, and reinforcing the idea that abilities can be developed through effort and persistence.

Mindset Reflection Questions:

- What story am I telling myself about my ability to succeed?

- Do I see challenges as threats or as opportunities to grow?

- What would I believe about myself if fear weren't holding me back?

The Power of Action

Action is the bridge between mindset and results. Without action, even the strongest belief system remains theory. Action requires commitment, consistency, and courage, especially when progress feels slow or resistance arises.

Tips for Effective Action:

1. Start Small: Break goals into manageable steps. Momentum grows with each success.

2. Consistent: Small, steady actions beat sporadic bursts of effort.

3. Track Progress: Celebrate milestones to reinforce motivation.

4. Stay Flexible: Adapt your actions when life changes but never stop moving forward.

How Mindset + Action Creates Results

Think of mindset as the *fuel* and action as the *engine*. Without fuel, the engine won't run; without an engine, fuel has no direction. Together, they generate results that create transformation.

Case Example:

- Client: Wants to launch a small business.

- Old Mindset: "I'm not smart enough to run my own company."

- New Mindset: "I can learn the skills I need to succeed."

- Actions: Enroll in a business course, research the market, draft a business plan, and network with mentors.

- Results: Within 12 months, the client successfully launched their business and gained confidence in their ability to grow it.

Coaching Insight

As a coach, my role is to support you, identify and strengthen your mindset while supporting you to take intentional action. The two together form a cycle:

- Mindset empowers action.

- Action reinforces mindset.

- Together, they create lasting results.

Key Takeaway: *When you shift your mindset and consistently take action, transformation becomes inevitable.*

5. Habit Formation: The 21/90 Rule

Our lives are built on habits. The small actions we repeat daily become the foundation of who we are and what we achieve. Transformation doesn't usually come from one grand event, it comes from consistent, intentional practices that compound over time. The 21/90 Rule is a powerful framework that helps us understand how to build habits that last.

This principle suggests:

- It takes 21 days of consistent practice to form a new habit.

- It takes 90 days of sustained effort for that habit to become a permanent lifestyle change.

By applying this rule, you can rewire your brain, reshape your routines, and create long-lasting behaviors that support your goals and dreams.

Why Habits Matter in Transformation

Habits are the invisible architecture of daily life. They influence how we think, act, and respond to challenges. A single new habit— such as exercising daily, practicing gratitude, or setting aside quiet time for reflection—can shift the trajectory of your health, relationships, and personal growth.

Yet building habits isn't just about discipline. It's about psychology. The brain thrives on patterns and repetition. Each time we repeat an action, we strengthen the neural pathways that make it easier to do again. Over time, habits move from conscious effort to automatic behavior.

The Science Behind 21/90

The 21-day phase is about breaking old patterns and rewiring the brain. This is often the hardest stage because your mind and body resist change.

- Example: Waking up early feels uncomfortable for the first 2–3 weeks.

The 90-day phase is about reinforcement. By continuing the habit beyond the initial period, it becomes ingrained as part of your identity.

- Example: After 3 months of waking up early, your body adjusts, and it becomes second nature.

Step-by-Step Guide to Applying the 21/90 Rule

Step 1: Choose One Habit at a Time

Avoid overwhelming yourself by trying to change too much. Focus on a single habit that will make the biggest impact.

- Example: "I will write in my gratitude journal every evening."

Step 2: Commit for 21 Days

Mark your calendar. Hold yourself accountable. The first 3 weeks are about consistency, not perfection.

- Example: Even if you can only write one sentence in your journal, do it daily.

Step 3: Extend to 90 Days

After the initial 21 days, recommit for 90 more. This is where discipline turns into identity.

- Example: By day 90, journaling has become part of your bedtime routine, like brushing your teeth.

Step 4: Track Progress

Use a journal, app, or accountability partner to celebrate milestones and notice patterns.

Step 5: Reward Yourself

Small celebrations reinforce progress. This isn't about indulgence—it's about acknowledging your growth.

Coaching Example

A client once came to me struggling with low self-confidence. She decided to start a simple habit: writing three things she was proud of each night.

- The first 21 days were challenging—she often forgot and sometimes struggled to think of even one positive thing.

- By day 45, she noticed her mindset shifting. She began recognizing wins in her daily life.

- By day 90, the practice felt natural, and her self-esteem had grown significantly. She no longer looked for reasons to feel unworthy; she was grounded in her progress.

Reflection Prompts
- What is one small habit that, if you practiced it daily, could transform your life?

- What obstacles might you face in the first 21 days? How will you handle them?

- What will your life look like 90 days from now if you commit to this habit?

Closing Thoughts

Habits are not about willpower—they are about systems. The 21/90 Rule is a framework that turns intention into transformation. Remember, you don't need to overhaul your entire life in one step. Focus on one change at a time and let consistency build momentum.

Key Takeaway: *The habits you form today will become the foundation of the life you live tomorrow. Commit for 21 days, sustain for 90, and watch transformation unfold.*

7. Mindfulness + Self-Compassion + Consistency

Transformation is not only about setting goals and pushing forward—it's also about how gently and consistently you walk the path. Many people begin their journeys with high energy, only to burn out when life gets difficult. What sustains transformation isn't force—it's a rhythm of *mindfulness, self-compassion, and consistency.*

These three elements form a cycle:

- Mindfulness keeps you present.
- Self-compassion helps you stay kind to yourself when you stumble.
- Consistency ensures small steps add up to big changes.

Together, they create a foundation for lasting growth.

The Role of Mindfulness

Mindfulness is the practice of being fully present in the moment, aware of your thoughts, feelings, and actions without judgment. It allows you to notice when you're aligned with your goals and when you're drifting away.

- Why it matters in coaching: Many clients struggle not because they don't know *what* to do, but because they aren't aware of *when* they get distracted or discouraged. Mindfulness shines a light on those moments.

- Practical applications: Deep breathing, journaling, meditation, and even mindful walking can help bring clarity and reduce stress.

Example: One of my clients, a busy mother and professional, found herself constantly overwhelmed. By practicing 10 minutes of mindful breathing each morning, she noticed she was less reactive during the day and made decisions with greater clarity.

The Role of Self-Compassion

Self-compassion is often the missing ingredient in personal growth. Too many people believe they can shame or criticize themselves for change, but harsh self-talk rarely builds lasting transformation—it builds fear and resentment.

- What it looks like: Speaking to yourself the way you would to a dear friend.

Instead of "I failed again," try "This was a tough day, but I am still learning."

- Why it matters: Without self-compassion, one mistake can spiral into self-sabotage. With it, you can pick yourself up, adjust, and keep moving.

Example: When I first began running, I often criticized myself for not being fast enough. Over time, I learned to say, "I showed up—that matters." That shift allowed me to keep going. Eventually, consistency—not speed—helped me reach my fitness goals.

The Power of Consistency
Consistency is where dreams become reality. Small, repeated actions compound into remarkable results. Yet consistency is only possible when paired with mindfulness and self-compassion.

- Consistency without mindfulness can turn into mindless repetition that leads nowhere.

- Consistency without self-compassion becomes punishment, which leads to burnout.

- But when combined, consistency becomes a joyful rhythm of progress.

Example: A client working on writing her first book committed to writing just 300 words per day. Some days she wrote more, some days less, but by being consistent, she had a full manuscript within a year.

Step-by-Step Application

Step 1: Begin with Awareness (Mindfulness)

- Ask yourself: *What am I feeling right now? What do I need most at this moment?*

- Practice daily check-ins. Even 2–3 minutes of mindful breathing before starting your day can reset your focus.

Step 2: Add Kindness (Self-Compassion)

- Replace self-criticism with self-kindness.

- Create affirmations like: *"I am allowed to be a work in progress."*

- Journal one way you showed up for yourself today.

Step 3: Anchor with Action (Consistency)

- Choose a small, repeatable habit aligned with your goal.

- Example: 10 minutes of walking or dancing, 5 minutes of journaling, or one gratitude note each evening.

- Track your actions, not your perfection.

Coaching Example

A young professional came to me frustrated about her lack of progress at work. She oscillated between bursts of productivity and long periods of avoidance. Through coaching, we built a framework:

- Mindfulness: She began noticing her trigger, emails from her boss made her feel anxious.

- Self-Compassion: Instead of berating herself for procrastinating, she acknowledged her fear and reminded herself that mistakes were part of learning.

- Consistency: She committed to responding to emails within 24 hours, no matter how small the step.

Within months, her confidence and performance improved—not because she worked harder, but because she worked with awareness, kindness, and steady consistency.

Reflection Prompts

1. When do you notice yourself being most critical of your progress?

2. How can you replace self-criticism with self-kindness in those moments?

3. What is one small action you could repeat daily for the next 30 days?

4. How might mindfulness help you recognize when you're slipping into old habits?

Closing Thoughts

Transformation doesn't come from perfection—it comes from progress. Mindfulness grounds you. Self-compassion strengthens you. Consistency carries you.

When these three practices work together, they create a sustainable path toward growth. You don't need to rush or punish yourself into change. Instead, you can build a life rooted in awareness, kindness, and steady, intentional action.

Key Takeaway: *Transformation is not about doing more. It's about doing the right things—mindfully, kindly, and consistently.*

8. The Pomodoro Technique: Mastering Time, One Interval at a Time

Time is one of the greatest equalizers in life—every person has the same twenty-four hours in a day. Yet why do some people seem to accomplish so much while others struggle to keep up? The answer is often not about working *harder* but about working *smarter*.

The Pomodoro Technique, created in the late 1980s by Francesco Cirillo, offers a deceptively simple but highly effective way of approaching tasks. The name comes from the Italian word *pomodoro* (tomato), inspired by the tomato-shaped kitchen timer Cirillo used as a student. At its core, this technique transforms overwhelming tasks into manageable sprints of focus and rest.

Rather than pushing yourself endlessly through long hours, the Pomodoro Technique encourages you to work in focused intervals, traditionally 25 minutes each, followed by a 5-minute break. After four intervals (or

"Pomodoros"), you take a longer break of 15–30 minutes.

This cycle creates a rhythm that honors both productivity and rest, making it easier to stay consistent, avoid burning out, and enjoy the work you do.

Why the Pomodoro Technique Works

- Beats Procrastination: large tasks often feel intimidating, leading to avoidance. By committing to just 25 minutes, the entry barrier feels lower, making it easier to get started.

- Harnesses Focus: When you know you only need to focus for a short burst, distractions feel less tempting. You're more likely to stay present and engaged.

- Respects Energy Cycles: The human brain struggles with prolonged focus. Regular breaks allow your mind to reset, preventing fatigue and improving long-term attention.

- Creates a Sense of Achievement; Each completed Pomodoro feels like a small win. These mini successes add up, reinforcing motivation and momentum.

Step-by-Step Guide

Step 1: Choose a Task
Pick something specific, like writing a report, answering emails, reading a chapter, or studying for an exam.

Step 2: Set a Timer
Traditionally, 25 minutes is the standard, but you can adjust it depending on your energy and the task. The key is commitment.

Step 3: Work Without Distractions
During this time, focus solely on your task. Silence notifications, close unrelated tabs, and give yourself permission to fully engage.

Step 4: Take a Short Break (5 minutes)
Stretch, walk around, hydrate, or breathe. The break resets your brain and prevents mental fatigue.

Step 5: After Four Pomodoros, take a Longer Break (15–30 minutes)

This deeper rest period gives your brain the chance to recharge, ensuring sustained focus throughout the day.

Coaching Example

A client of mine, a graduate student writing her thesis, was overwhelmed by the scale of the project. She often stared at her laptop for hours, making little progress. We introduced the Pomodoro Technique:

- She committed to writing for just 25 minutes at a time.

- After each session, she stretched, drank water, and gave herself permission to rest.

- Within weeks, she had built a consistent routine, writing nearly 1,000 words per day.

What once felt impossible became achievable—simply by breaking it into intervals.

Customizing the Pomodoro Technique

One of the strengths of this method is its flexibility. While 25 minutes is standard, it can be adapted:

- For Deep Work: Extend to 45–50 minutes if you're doing highly creative or focused tasks.

- For Beginners: Start with 15–20 minutes to build focus gradually.

- For Teams: Use synchronized Pomodoros during co-working sessions to boost collective productivity.

The key is to honor both the *work interval* and the *break interval*. Skipping breaks can undermine the entire system.

Common Challenges & Solutions
- "I keep getting interrupted."

- Solution: Use Cirillo's "inform, negotiate, and call back" rule. Let people know you're in a focus session, schedule a time to reconnect, and return to your task.

- "25 minutes feels too short for me." Solution: Experiment with longer sessions. Some people thrive with a 50/10 rhythm (50 minutes work, 10 minutes rest).

- "I lose momentum during breaks." Solution: Keep breaks active but brief. Avoid social media or long distractions that pull you too far away from your task.

Coaching Applications

The Pomodoro Technique is especially effective for:

- Clients with procrastination struggles – It lowers resistance to starting.

- Busy professionals – Helps structure chaotic days into manageable focus sessions.

- Students – Builds focus and study habits while reducing exam stress.

- Creatives – Provides structure for long, unstructured projects like writing, painting, or music composition.

Reflection Prompts

◆ What tasks in your life currently feel too overwhelming to start?

◆ How might breaking them into 25-minute intervals shift your perspective?

◆ When do you notice your energy starting to dip during the day? How can breaks be built around that natural rhythm?

◆ If you customized your Pomodoro length, what timing would best suit your lifestyle?

Closing Thoughts

The Pomodoro Technique is more than a time-management tool—it's a practice of *self-awareness, rhythm, and respect for your energy.* It teaches you that productivity does not require endless hours of pushing through. Instead, it's about intentional focus, followed by intentional rest.

By mastering time in intervals, you reclaim control over your day. Instead of being consumed by deadlines and distractions, you can build a steady rhythm that leads to progress, clarity, and fulfillment.

Key Takeaway: *Productivity is not about doing more, it's about doing the right things with presence, rhythm, and energy. The Pomodoro Technique offers exactly that.*

Top of Form/Bottom of Form
9. Journaling and Reflection

Words have power. Writing allows clients to process emotions, explore beliefs, and articulate their dreams. I often provide reflective prompts such as: *"What does my ideal life look like?"* or *"What belief is holding me back from stepping into my full potential?"* Journaling becomes a sacred space where self-discovery takes root.

Conclusion

Each of these tools is like a brushstroke on the canvas of your life. They help bring depth, color, and texture to the picture you are painting. Used consistently, they create momentum, helping you move steadily toward transformation.

For more information, please visit my website: www.tlifecoachinggrief.com

Chapter 4: Dreams Like Mine – Aspirations, Ambitions, and Goals

"Dreams are not illusions; they are sacred invitations to become who you are meant to be."
-Antoinette A. Enohmbi

The Role of Dreams in Our Lives

Dreams are the language of possibility. They speak to us in whispers, in visions, in restless stirrings that tug at our hearts. Whether they come as vivid night visions or as quiet longings during the day, dreams are God-given gifts that help us understand ourselves and the path before us. They also refer to your aspirations, ambitions, and goals that you deeply desire to achieve. In this setting, they are called dreams in life.

Dreams serve many purposes in our lives:

1. Roadmap of life
   Aspirations, ambitions, and goals provide purpose, direction, and motivation, helping us focus on what truly matters to create a more fulfilling life. They act as a roadmap, dividing consistent action, strengthening resilience, and fostering personal

growth by inspiring us to achieve larger visions and make meaningful contributions.

2. Emotional Processor: Dreams help us release emotions we might be holding inside. Sometimes, after a long day of stress or after a painful season, we dream of scenarios that help us process anger, grief, or unspoken desires. The subconscious mind has a way of working while our bodies rest, sorting through feelings that we may not have words for.

3. Problem-Solvers: Our waking minds can get trapped by logic, but dreams bypass those limits. They often weave together images and metaphors that point us toward creative solutions. How many times have you woken up with clarity about a problem that felt unsolvable the night before? Dreams open the door to new ways of thinking.

4. Reflective Mirrors: Dreams mirror our inner world. They reflect the conflicts we wrestle with, the hopes we carry quietly, and the fears we may try to push away.

When we take time to reflect on our dreams, we often discover truths about ourselves we didn't know were there.

5. Healing and Growth Tools: Dreams can help us integrate our experiences—especially the difficult ones. They allow us to revisit memories, process emotions, and gently move toward healing. A dream may not erase our pain, but it can provide a safe inner space to begin working through it.

6. Spiritual Guides: Beyond psychology, dreams can also serve as spiritual invitations. Throughout Scripture, God has spoken through dreams—guiding Joseph to flee with Mary and baby Jesus or revealing the future to prophets and kings. Dreams can carry messages from God, nudging us to pay attention, change direction, or to prepare for something greater.

When we understand dreams in this broad sense, they cease to be random nighttime images or fanciful wishes. They become tools for growth, self-discovery, healing, and spiritual guidance.

Dreams as Aspirations: The Desires of the Heart

When most people talk about "dreams," they aren't referring to the visions that come in the night. They're talking about life dreams—our deepest aspirations, ambitions, and goals. These are the visions of the lives we long to live:

- The dream of starting a business.

- The dream of raising a loving family.

- The dream of traveling the world.

- The dream of healing from grief and living with joy again.

- The dream of discovering our God-given purpose and living it fully.

These kinds of dreams are not just about wishful thinking. They are a compass for our lives. They give us direction, motivation, and hope. In fact, without dreams, life can feel empty—like a ship drifting without a destination.

When I was younger, I used to define success by external achievements: grades, awards, or recognition. I thought the more certificates I collected, the more worthy I would be. But through self-reflection, coaching, and spiritual direction, I realized that true success is not about chasing validation—it's about aligning with God's purpose for my life and creating a future that feels authentic and fulfilling.

Dreams as aspirations are the blueprint for that future. They remind us that we were not placed on this earth to simply exist, but to grow, to contribute, and to live with meaning.

How to Pursue and Achieve Your Dreams

Dreams can sometimes feel overwhelming, especially when they seem too big, too far, or too unrealistic. That's why breaking them down into smaller, intentional steps is so important. Here are some key principles I share with my clients when guiding them toward their dreams:

1. Clarify Your Dream

- Ask yourself: *What do I truly want in life?* Is it peace, purpose, financial freedom, or deeper relationships?

- Write your dream down in detail. Imagine yourself living it. What does it look like? What does it feel like? Who is with you?

- The clearer your dream, the more powerful it can guide your actions.

2. Break It into Goals

- Dreams are big and sometimes vague, but goals are specific.

- Example: "If your dream is to write a book, set a goal to write 500 words a day, or to complete your first draft in six months."

- Small steps, done consistently, build momentum.

3. Use the SMART Framework

Example: If you desire a promotion at work

- S – Specific: Define exactly what you want.

    - Clearly define what promotion means to you
    - Example: "I want to be promoted to senior project manager within the next six months."

- M – Measurable: Create ways to track your progress.

    - Example: "I will track my performance reviews, meet regularly with my manager to discuss progress, and take on two additional projects per quarter."

- A – Achievable: Is this goal realistic? What resources do you have?

    - Example: "I have the skills and experience needed for the role, but I need to improve my leadership and time management skills."

- R – Relevant: Make sure your goals align with your values and vision.

    - Why does this goal matter to you?

- Example: "A promotion will help me advance my career, increase my salary, and allow me to take on more responsibility, which aligns with my long-term career goals."

- T – Time-bound: Set a deadline to hold yourself accountable.

  Example: "I want to be promoted within six months, by February 2026"

4. Create a Plan of Action

- List the steps you need to take, no matter how small.

- Identify resources—people, courses, mentors, or tools—that can support your journey.

- Schedule time to work on your dream. Dreams grow in the soil of discipline.

5. Expect Obstacles

- Setbacks are not signs of failure; they are invitations to learn.

- Instead of asking, *"Why me?"* ask, *"What is this teaching me?"*

- Build resilience by practicing patience, faith, and self-compassion when challenges arise.

6. Celebrate the Small Victories

- Every step forward is progress. Celebrate it.

- Gratitude fuels perseverance. Acknowledge how far you've come, not just how far you still have to go.

The 5 W's: A Roadmap to Your Goals

To make dreams real, clarity is essential. One of the tools I often share with clients is **the 5 W's**, a simple but powerful framework that brings structure to your goals and helps you move from vision to action.

1. <u>Who</u>? Who is this dream for? Who benefits when you take this step— yourself, your family, your community, or the world?

2. <u>What</u>? What is the specific dream or goal? What exactly do you want to achieve, and how will you know when you've achieved it?

3. <u>When</u>? When will you act? What is your timeline? Dreams need deadlines to become reality.

4. <u>Where</u>? Where will this dream come to life? Is it tied to a physical location, like moving to a new city or opening a local business? Or is it a dream of the heart, meant to be lived out anywhere?

5. <u>Why</u>? Why does this dream matter to you? Why is it worth your time, energy, and sacrifice? This "why" is what fuels your commitment when things get hard.

By asking yourself these questions, you begin to turn your dreams from abstract desires into a clear, practical, and spiritually aligned vision.

When Night Dreams Speak into Life Dreams

Earlier, I spoke about literal dreams that visit us while we sleep. At first glance, they may seem disconnected from our daily goals and ambitions. But often, these dreams are deeply intertwined with our life journey.

- Dreams of success or failure may reflect your deep desires or your hidden fears. A dream of standing on a stage, speaking confidently, might be God's way of affirming your potential. A dream of stumbling or falling might be an invitation to face your fear of failure and trust God more fully.

- Dreams of personal growth can mirror what your soul is yearning for. Dreams of climbing a mountain may represent the challenges you are ready to face. Dreams of being lost may point to the need for guidance or clarity.

- Dreams as divine whispers often remind us that God speaks in ways beyond words. In the Bible, Joseph received direction through dreams, and Daniel interpreted dreams that shaped nations.

In our own lives, God may be using dreams to prepare us for something ahead or to reveal truths we need to embrace.

For me, dreams have always been both mysteries and teachers. They have given me insights into my own life and, at times, offered guidance for others. They have deepened my faith by reminding me that God is always near, weaving His presence into both my waking and sleeping hours.

Reflection Prompts:
Take 10 minutes to reflect on your own dreams, both the ones that visit you at night and the ones you hold in your heart. Journal your responses to these prompts:

1. What is one dream you've had while sleeping that still lingers with you today? What might it be trying to tell you?

2. What is a life dream or aspiration that excites you, even if it feels far away or impossible right now?

3. When you think about your goals, can you identify your "why"? Why does this dream matter to you?

4. What small steps could you take this week to move closer to one of your dreams?

5. How might you use your dreams, literal or aspirational—to guide you toward growth and transformation?

Closing Invitation

Dreams are not accidents. They are signposts. They are gentle reminders of who we are and what we can become. They carry our emotions, our hopes, and sometimes even God's whispers.

As your coach, I want to help you bring your dreams closer—to bridge the gap between where you desire to be. You are capable of more than you realize. Your dreams are not foolish, too late, or too far out of reach. They are the seeds of your future.

Together, we will nurture those seeds. We will clarify your goals, identify your strengths, and build a pathway toward the life you were created to live. Remember: your dreams are not distant stars; they are closer than you think.

Reflection Question: What aspirational dreams do you have that you are ready to pursue?

Chapter 5: Mastery of Life – Personal Growth, Relationships, and NLP

"True mastery is not about controlling life but about learning to dance with it—gracefully, faithfully, and authentically."

-Antoinette A. Enohmbi

What Does It Mean to Master Life?

When people hear the word "mastery," they sometimes think of perfection—never making mistakes, always being in control. But mastery of life is not about flawless living. It is about cultivating wisdom, resilience, and balance so that no matter what storms arise, you can navigate them with strength and grace.

Life mastery means becoming deeply aware of who you are, aligning your choices with your values, and living with a sense of purpose. It is the opposite of living on autopilot. Instead of being swept along by circumstances, you learn to respond intentionally. You begin to move through life not as a victim of fate but as an active participant in your own story.

I often compare life mastery to sailing a ship. You cannot control the wind or the waves, but you can learn to steer, to adjust your sails, and to trust the compass guiding you.

The Foundations of Mastery
There are several pillars that support the journey toward mastery. Each one is interconnected, and together they form a solid foundation for growth.

1. Self-Awareness
Everything begins here. You cannot change what you do not see. Self-awareness is the ability to notice your thoughts, emotions, and behaviors without judgment. It's about asking: *What motivates me? What patterns am I repeating? What values truly matter to me?*

Practices like journaling, prayer, and mindfulness help you build this awareness. For me, silence and spiritual direction became powerful tools that allowed me to hear not only my inner voice, but also God's gentle whisper.

2. Emotional Mastery
Life mastery requires learning to manage emotions rather than letting emotions manage you. This doesn't mean suppressing feelings

but understanding them. When you feel anger, grief, or fear, can you pause and ask what it is trying to teach you?

Techniques like breathwork, meditation, and positive reframing allow us to regulate emotions. NLP (Neuro-Linguistic Programming) tools, for instance, can help reprogram negative thought patterns into empowering ones.

3. Resilience and Adaptability

No one escapes hardship. Illness, loss, disappointment, or unexpected change will come. Mastery means cultivating resilience— the ability to bounce back and adapt. Each setback becomes not the end of your story but a stepping stone toward greater strength.

When my father battled cancer, I felt like my world was collapsing. Yet it was during that season that I discovered resilience I didn't know I had. Caring for him while also raising my children tested me in ways I could never have prepared for, but it also revealed my capacity to endure, to love, and to grow.

4. Purpose and Meaning

Without purpose, mastery feels empty. Purpose is what gives direction to our choices and energy to our actions. It doesn't always come as one grand calling; often it shows up in small daily decisions—choosing kindness over bitterness, service over self, forgiveness over resentment.

When we live with purpose, we walk in alignment with our true self.

5. Relationships and Connection

Life mastery is not a solo project. It is lived out in community, through relationships that challenge and nurture us. Empathy, forgiveness, and authentic communication are essential.

I've seen clients experience breakthroughs simply by learning to listen differently—to themselves, to their loved ones, and to others. Relationships are often the mirror that shows us who we are becoming.

Tools for Mastery: NLP and Beyond

One of the most practical tools I use in my coaching is Neuro-Linguistic Programming (NLP). NLP is based on the idea that our thoughts, language, and behaviors are interconnected. By changing how we think and speak, we can change how we feel and act.

Some simple NLP strategies include:

- Anchoring: Linking a positive state (like confidence or peace) to a specific gesture or word so you can recall it in difficult moments.

- Reframing: Choosing to see challenges in a new light. Instead of *"I failed,"* you reframe it as *"I learned something valuable."*

- Visualization: Mentally rehearsing success, whether it's speaking confidently, navigating a hard conversation, or pursuing a dream.

NLP has given many of my clients tools to break free from fear, heal from limiting beliefs, and step into new possibilities. Combined with Silence, Reflection, and Introspection, it creates a holistic pathway to transformation.

Stories of Mastery in Action

One client came to me feeling overwhelmed by her career. She had lost passion for her work and felt stuck, but leaving seemed terrifying. Through our sessions, she discovered her true value: creativity, service, and freedom—and realized her current job didn't reflect them. Together, we used NLP visualization to imagine her thriving in a new role. Step by step, she gained the courage to transition into a field that aligned with her purpose.

Another client struggled with unresolved grief. He carried anger that seeped into his relationships. Using reflection, journaling, and reframing, he learned to see grief not as a weight to bury but as a doorway to healing. His relationships deepened, and he began to live with more compassion for himself and others.

Mastery does not mean life becomes easy. It means you learn to meet life's challenges with courage, clarity, and hope.

Reflection Prompts:

♦ Where in your life do you feel "stuck," and how might greater self-awareness help you move forward?

♦ What emotions tend to overwhelm you? How can you begin to practice emotional mastery in those moments?

♦ Think about a time you showed resilience. What did you learn about yourself?

♦ What values matter most to you, and how well does your current life align with them?

♦ Who in your life helps you become your best self? How can you nurture those relationships more intentionally?

Closing Invitation

Mastering life is not about having all the answers, it is about learning to ask the right questions, to live with hope, and to keep moving forward even when the path is unclear. It is about becoming both student and teacher on your own journey.

Tony Robbins is a best-selling American author, motivational speaker, and life and business coach and strategist. When I read his book, *"Unlimited Power"* years ago, I was struck by how much it echoed lessons I had already learned: we have the power to reprogram our minds, to shift our focus, and to change our outcomes. Later, I was introduced to the work of Mel Robbins, who, like Tony Robbins, is a well-known motivational speaker and coach. When I read Mel's *"The High 5 Habit,"* I was reminded that mastery is not just about discipline—it is also about self-love, kindness, and celebration.

My father's example of forgiveness and generosity continues to inspire me. His life showed me that mastery is not found in status or control but in humility, kindness, and the ability to connect with people at every level of society.

As your coach, I want you to know this: you already carry within you the seeds of mastery, and through intentional practice, reflection, and introspection, those seeds can grow into a life marked by resilience, clarity, and purpose.

Reflection Question: What does life mastery look like for you, and what is one step you can take today to move closer to it?

Chapter 6: Health and Wellness – Nurturing the Body, Mind, and Spirit

"Wellness is not a destination but a daily choice—to honor your body, renew your mind, and align your spirit with what gives you life."
— Antoinette A. Enohmbi.

The Wholeness of Health and Wellness

When most people hear the word *health*, they immediately think of physical fitness, medical checkups, or eating vegetables. While these are vital, health is not just about whether our body feels strong or free of disease. True health is holistic. It encompasses our physical, emotional, mental, and spiritual well-being.

Wellness is not a destination you arrive at one day and say, *"Now I am healthy forever."* Rather, it is a journey, a way of living, and a daily practice of caring for yourself so you can live a meaningful, balanced, and joyful life.

For me, health and wellness became deeply personal after moving to the United States and later, during my father's illness. Balancing motherhood, my professional responsibilities, and caregiving for my father forced me to face my limits. I realized that to be present for others, I needed to nurture myself in body, mind, and spirit. This realization shaped not only how I lived, but also how I coach others.

1. Physical Health – Caring for your body

Physical health is not about perfection or achieving a certain body type. It is about strengthening our bodies so that we can show up fully for life.

Key Practices for Physical Health:

- Movement: Regular physical activity keeps your heart healthy, strengthens your muscles, and boosts your energy. This doesn't mean you need to run a marathon. It can be as simple as walking, dancing, stretching, or playing with your children. For me, volleyball was my way of finding freedom in my youth, and later, running half-marathons became both a physical challenge and a spiritual release.

- Nutrition: What we eat fuels our body and mind. Choosing whole, nourishing foods is a way of respecting the vessel God has given us. I encourage my clients to approach food with gratitude instead of guilt. Instead of saying, *"I can't have this,"* shift to *"I choose foods that support my body and my goals."*

- Rest and Renewal: We live in a culture that glorifies busyness, but the human body was not designed for constant activity. Sleep is sacred—it allows our body to repair, our mind to process, and our soul to be still. I remember when my children were young, I often sacrificed sleep to keep up with responsibilities, only to find myself overwhelmed and depleted. I had to learn that rest is not laziness; it is stewardship of life.

- Health Care Engagement: Your body is your lifelong companion—treat it with care. Stay connected with your healthcare provider, not only when you're unwell but through regular wellness checkups. Listening to your body and following your provider's recommendations are powerful acts of self-respect and self-love.

Reflection Prompt:
What small step can you take today to honor your body? Could it be drinking more water,

eating more fruit and vegetables, walking outside, or simply resting without guilt?

2. Emotional and Mental Health – Healing the Inner World

Our inner world—our thoughts, emotions, and beliefs—shapes how we experience life. You can be physically fit but weighed down by stress, anxiety, guilt, or unprocessed grief. This is why emotional and mental health are just as essential to holistic wellness.

Building Emotional Resilience:
Resilience is not about avoiding pain but about learning to rise again after challenges. When my father was sick, there were days I wanted to collapse under the weight of fear and grief. But it was in those moments, when I turned to God and permitted myself to *feel*, that I discovered my strength.

Tools for Emotional Wellness:
- Mindfulness & Presence: Taking deep breaths, meditating, or pausing to notice your surroundings can reduce anxiety and bring you back into the present moment.

- Journaling: Writing down your thoughts is a powerful way to release emotions and uncover patterns. Many clients discover hidden beliefs about themselves when they put words to their feelings.

- Healthy Boundaries: Emotional wellness also means knowing when to say *no* and when to step back. A dear client once carried the guilt of setting boundaries with her brother, who struggled with addiction. Through our sessions, she learned that protecting her mental health was not abandonment but an act of love for herself and her family.

Reflection Prompt:
What emotions do you often suppress? How might acknowledging them, instead of avoiding them, help you heal and grow?

3. Spiritual Health – Rooted in God's Presence

Spiritual health is the grounding force of my life and my work. It is about more than religion; it is about cultivating a deep awareness of God's presence in all things.

As a young girl, I grew up with the image of God as a strict judge, always watching and keeping a record of my mistakes. That view made me cautious, fearful, and hesitant to open my heart fully. It wasn't until my mid-thirties, during my formation program in spiritual direction, that I discovered a new image of God. William Barry's book *A Friendship Like No Other* taught me that God desires an intimate friendship with us. In his other book, *God and You: Prayer as a Personal Relationship*, Barry reminded me that there is no single "right" way to pray. God simply longs for our presence, our honesty, our laughter, our tears, and our gratitude.

This revelation changed everything for me. I began to see prayer not as a ritual to earn God's love, but as a conversation with a friend who already loves me. That shift gave me peace and helped me embrace the fullness of my identity in Christ.

Practices for Nurturing Spiritual Wellness:

- Prayer as Conversation: Talk to God honestly about your fears, joys, doubts, and dreams.

- Silence and Stillness: Spend time in quiet, allowing God's presence to wash over you.

- Gratitude Practice: Each day, write down three things you are grateful for, and thank God for them. Gratitude shifts our perspective from scarcity to abundance.

- Spiritual Direction: A spiritual director or companion can walk with you on your journey, helping you discern God's presence and voice in your daily life. And you can also seek support and guidance where you feel the most comfortable.

Reflection Prompt:
How do you currently experience God's presence in your life? What might change if you began to see Him not only as a distant authority but as a close and loving friend?

4. Living Well Through Balance
Health and wellness are sustained when balance is embraced. Balance does not mean splitting time evenly between work, family, faith, and rest—it means being attentive to what your life is calling for in each season. Some seasons may require more energy devoted to family, while others may call you to focus on your career, health, or spiritual growth.

For me, balance has often been about releasing the unrealistic expectation that I could "do it all." When my children were younger, I struggled with the idea of not being enough. I thought that if I just pushed harder, worked later, or carried more responsibility, I could hold everything together. But eventually, I learned that real strength doesn't come from doing it all—it comes from knowing when to ask for help, when to pause, and when to rest in God's presence.

Balance is also about integrating joy into daily life. Joy is not a reward for achieving all your goals; it is available in the small, ordinary moments—a family dinner, a walk in the park, a smile from a stranger. When you choose to notice and celebrate these moments, you are practicing wellness in its purest form.

Reflection Prompt:
Where in your life do you need more balance right now? Is it in your time, your energy, your relationships, or your spiritual practices?

5. The Lifelong Journey of Wellness
Health and wellness are not quick fixes; they are lifelong commitments. Just as seasons change, our needs shift over time. In our

twenties, we may focus on building careers and exploring our identities. In midlife, we may be balancing career, family, and caregiving, often wrestling with fatigue or burnout. Later in life, we may face the grief of aging, learning to let go of former capabilities while embracing the wisdom and perspective that comes with maturity.

Wellness is about adapting to each of these seasons with grace. It is about asking: *What does my body need right now? What does my mind need? What does my soul need?*

When I look back at my journey—from childhood in Cameroon, to my college years in the United States, to the years of raising children while caring for my father—I see a thread of resilience and faith that carried me through. I also see how wellness requires both discipline and compassion. There were days when I had to push myself to go outside for a walk even when I felt exhausted. And there were days when I had to let myself rest and be still, trusting that God was working in me even when I wasn't "doing."

Practical Steps for Your Own Journey:

1. Start Small, Start Today: Choose one simple wellness habit to commit to this week, whether drinking more water, stretching for 10 minutes, or praying each morning.

2. Check Your Balance: Look at your life as a wheel. Which areas—physical, emotional, mental, spiritual, relational—feel full? Which feels neglected?

3. Celebrate Progress: Don't only celebrate big milestones. Honor the small steps: the walk you took, the meal you cooked, the prayer you whispered.

4. Invite God In: Remember, you don't walk this journey alone. God is Emmanuel, always with you. Invite him into every area of your awareness.

Closing Reflection

Health and wellness are sacred gifts, but they require our participation. You have been given one body, one mind, and one soul—each deserving of care, attention, and love. True transformation begins when you honor all three and recognize that they are interconnected.

Reflection Questions:

- What does health mean to you personally?

- In what ways do you already honor your body, mind, and spirit?

- Where might God be inviting you to slow down, to heal, or to grow?

- What new wellness practice could you begin today that would bring you closer to balance?

Chapter 7: Grief Coaching – Understanding and Living with Grief

Grief reveals the depth of our love. By allowing ourselves to feel, we also allow ourselves to heal."

— *Antoinette A. Enohmbi*

What Is Grief?

Grief is not something that can be fixed. It is not a problem to solve, but a natural and deep human response to the loss of someone or something precious to us. It may show up as sadness, anger, confusion, guilt, or even relief. Grief is as unique as a fingerprint—no two people experience it in the same way. Our relationship with the person or situation we lost, our cultural upbringing, our personality, and our coping mechanisms all shape how we grieve.

Grieving, though painful, is a healthy and necessary process. It gives us space to adapt to change, to honor what has been lost, and to begin the long journey from pain to healing, and eventually, to gratitude.

My journey into grief coaching was born out of personal experience. When my father was diagnosed with cancer, I became his primary caregiver. It was one of the hardest and most tender times of my life. At that time, I did not know what a grief coach was. I had a spiritual director, who was helpful, but I often found myself overwhelmed with emotions I could not name. I was on autopilot, caring for my father while raising three young children and managing a household. Inside, I was consumed by sadness, anger, and fear. It wasn't until later that I learned the name for what I had been experiencing: anticipatory grief—grieving the loss of someone before they are gone.

Realizing this was like finding language for a pain I had been carrying silently. It also revealed to me how important it is for people to have compassionate, informed support during grief. That discovery became the seed of my calling to become a grief coach.

The Many Faces of Grief
One of the most important truths I emphasize in grief coaching is this: grief does not look the same for everyone. There is no single path, no one-size-fits-all process. Individuals

experience grief in unique ways and should be respected as long as it's not harmful to them or others. Unfortunately, not everyone respects and understands that; for example, I was criticized by a family member regarding my grieving process following the loss of my father. Understanding the different types of grief helps us honor the wide range of human experiences.

1. Normal (Uncomplicated) Grief

This is the typical emotional reaction to loss—feelings of sadness, longing, disbelief, or even anger. Over time, the intensity softens, and people slowly adjust to life without what or whom they lost. This was the grief I experienced after my father's passing, and I am still walking the path from grief toward gratitude.

2. Anticipatory Grief

This begins before the loss itself, often when a loved one faces a terminal illness. It can stir sadness, anxiety, and even guilt as we begin to process what is coming. For me, it showed up during my father's illness. Even with the support of my mom, surrounded by family and friends, I felt like I was carrying the weight alone because I didn't know how to name or process what I was experiencing.

3. **Complicated Grief (Prolonged Grief Disorder)**
This occurs when grief remains intense and disruptive for an extended time, leaving a person feeling stuck in sorrow. For example, a widow who cannot move forward after the sudden death of her spouse may withdraw from others, struggle to function, and feel as though life has no meaning. In such cases, professional help is essential.

4. **Disenfranchised Grief**
Sometimes society does not recognize or validate certain kinds of loss. This could be the death of a pet, the loss of a pregnancy, or the ending of a non-traditional relationship. In many cultures—including my African context—miscarriage is rarely spoken about and often considered taboo. I remember a childhood friend who only learned in adulthood that her mother had miscarried years before she was

born. Her mother felt ashamed to share the story with others because the culture doesn't encourage such conversations. The women who go through such experiences are expected to move on as if nothing happened and not talk about it. The silence around it left my friend stunned. So many women carry this kind of grief silently, without acknowledgement or support.

5. Cumulative Grief

When multiple losses occur in a short period, grief layers upon itself. It becomes difficult to process one loss before another arrives. My family experienced this several years ago when my grandmother passed away, and the very next day her son—my uncle— suddenly died. The weight of losing two beloved family members so close together was devastating, and grief felt heavier than ever. When the deceased were presented for viewing, describing the scene as anything less than profoundly sad would be an understatement.

6. Delayed Grief

Sometimes grief does not show up right away. A person may feel the need to stay strong for others, or the reality of the loss may take time to sink in. I recalled a friend whose father passed away, and she immediately threw herself into funeral arrangements, managing the logistics both in the U.S. and back in Cameroon. She barely shed a tear, telling me, "I don't know how I feel." It was only months later, with the help of a grief coach, that she allowed herself to fully grieve.

7. Masked Grief

This occurs when grief hides behind other behaviors—anger, constant busyness, physical symptoms, or even forced cheerfulness. The person may not even realize their behavior is grief related. Sometimes, masking grief feels safer than reliving trauma or exposing vulnerability, but it eventually surfaces in other ways.

8. Ambiguous Grief

Ambiguous grief arises when loss is unclear. It may be physical—when someone disappears, such as in cases of kidnapping—or psychological, when a loved one is physically present but emotionally or cognitively absent, as with dementia. Without closure, this type of grief can feel like an endless cycle.

9. **Exaggerated Grief**
This is grief that intensifies beyond what is typical, often after multiple traumatic losses. It can manifest as overwhelming sorrow, self-destructive behaviors, chronic depression, or irrational fears. When grief remains debilitating for over a year, immediate professional help is necessary. Here are some signs to look out for.

*Overwhelming sorrow and feeling stuck in the grieving process
*Self-destructive behavior like substance abuse, suicidal thoughts, or nightmares
*Developing irrational fears
*Chronic depression
*Emotional outbursts and becoming overly emotional

10. The Grief of Aging

Aging brings its own unique grief. It is not about death, but about the loss of physical abilities, vitality, or independence. I remember when I began experiencing menopause without realizing it. I would feel hot in the evenings and didn't understand why. When my doctor explained it (hot flashes), I felt grief—grief for a body transitioning into a new season. Later, as an avid runner, I noticed I could no longer run a half-marathon with ease and at my normal pace. Even a 5K required a knee brace. These changes were reminders that life moves in seasons, and part of aging gracefully is learning to acknowledge and accept these shifts with compassion.

11. Absent Grief

Sometimes a person shows no visible signs of grief. They may be in denial or avoiding their feelings. While it may appear that they are coping, unresolved grief can surface as insomnia, heart palpitations, or disconnection from relationships. This type of grief is not healthy and often requires professional support.

Why Do We Grieve?

We grieve because we love. Love creates deep bonds, and when those bonds are broken—through death, separation, or change—our hearts naturally ache. Grief is the alarm system that signals the reality of loss and the need to adapt to a new way of being in the world.

When we allow ourselves to grieve fully, we clear our hearts and minds of the heavy weight of guilt, resentment, pain, or regret. One of my clients lost her brother to addiction, and she felt guilty for setting boundaries with him when his behavior became destructive. Through grief coaching, she learned to see that boundaries were not acts of rejection but acts of love and self-preservation. As she released her guilt, she was able to grieve honestly and eventually move toward peace.

For me, the grief of losing my father was initially unbearable. I could not imagine life without hearing his voice or seeing his face. I felt as though my world had ended, but with time, support, and guidance from my spiritual director, I discovered that grief does not freeze life; it reshapes it. Slowly, I began moving from grief to gratitude, learning to carry my father's memory in a way that gave me strength.

Grief also helps us reconstruct our identity. Each loss reshapes who we are, teaching us resilience, compassion, and a deeper understanding of life's fragility. By walking through grief rather than avoiding it, we create space for healing and transformation.

Grief and Culture

While grief is universal, the way it is expressed and processed is deeply influenced by culture, religion, and community. Different traditions shape how we mourn, how long grief is expected to last, and how emotions are expressed.

In many African and Eastern European cultures, grief is communal. Families and communities gather, share rituals, and carry the burden together. By contrast, in much of the Western world, grief is seen as a private matter, with individuals expected to "move on" quickly.

The level of emotional expression also varies. In the Yoruba tribe of Nigeria, for instance, parents are discouraged from attending their child's funeral or even seeing the body as an act of cultural restraint. In my Cameroonian culture, crying loudly during funerals is often discouraged. When my father passed away, I wept openly. I remember women coming to tell me to stop, insisting my tears would disturb his soul's peaceful departure. Their words pierced me because for me, crying was not a sign of weakness but a way to release the pain. Yet their reaction reflected deeply ingrained cultural beliefs.

Another cultural expectation placed on African men is that they must remain stoic. Vulnerability, especially in grief, is often seen as weakness.

Cultural practices around grief can sometimes leave people carrying unprocessed emotions, locked away by silence or societal pressure. That is why grief coaching is so important: it offers a safe, nonjudgmental space to express what culture might suppress. If you feel weighed down by unacknowledged grief, I encourage you to seek support.

Grief Coaching vs. Grief Therapy
Though grief coaching and grief therapy both offer support, they serve different purposes:

Grief Coaching-
Future-focused:

- Begins with where you are now and emphasizes self-knowledge, growth, and moving forward.

- Seeks to move a client from functioning to flourishing.

- Assumes the client is not broken but full of potential. Coaches cannot diagnose or prescribe medication.

- Action-oriented: focuses on behavior, mindset, and creating practical steps.

- Can lead to significant breakthroughs in a shorter time frame.

- Helps clients honor their loved ones by building extraordinary lives.

- Flexible and convenient: can be done in person, over the phone, or virtually.

- Asks the question: *"What's next?"*

Grief Therapy
- Past-focused: explores unresolved feelings about the lost person or situation.

- Seeks to move a patient from non-functioning to functioning.

- Therapists can diagnose mental health conditions and prescribe or coordinate treatment.

- Emotion-focused: emphasizes processing deep pain and trauma.

- Typically long-term and insight-oriented.

- Licensed and regulated by state laws, usually requiring in-person sessions.

- Asks the question: *"Why?"*

Both approaches have value, but they are distinct. Grief coaching does not replace therapy. Instead, it complements it, offering a forward-looking, empowering path for those who are ready to embrace healing and growth.

Reflection Prompts

- 1. Which type of grief resonates most with your personal experience?
- 2. How has your culture or community shaped the way you grieve?
- What practices help you process grief in a healthy way?
- Where in your grief journey could a grief coach support you?
- How might moving from grief to gratitude change the way you live today?

Closing Thoughts

Grief is one of the deepest reminders of our humanity. It shows us the depth of our love, the fragility of life, and the resilience of the human spirit. While grief is universal, the journey through it is profoundly personal. You do not have to walk this path alone. Whether through the companionship of a spiritual director, the support of a grief coach, or the care of a therapist, healing becomes possible when we allow ourselves to be seen, heard, and held.

As your grief coach, I want to walk alongside you—not to take away your pain, but to help you carry it, name it, and transform it. Together, we can move toward healing, toward gratitude, and toward a life that honors both what has been lost and what remains.

Reflection questions:

How can you honor your loss while opening your heart to new possibilities of life, love, and growth?

Chapter 8: God's Presence in Our Journey – Love, Faith, Dreams, and Spiritual Growth

"When we surrender our plans to God's presence, we discover that love carries us, faith fuels us, and dreams become pathways to spiritual growth."

— *Antoinette A. Enohmbi*

God's Presence in Our Journey

From the moment we take our first breath to the final chapter of our lives, God's presence surrounds us. It is not always loud or dramatic—more often, it is quiet, subtle, and deeply intimate. In the stillness of the night, in the chaos of parenting, in the silence of grief, and in the joy of accomplishment, God is there.

The scriptures remind us that God is both transcendent, existing beyond time and space, and immanent, dwelling with us in our everyday lives. *"Do I not fill heaven and earth?" declares the Lord* (Jeremiah 23:24). That means we don't have to strive to "find" God in some faraway place. He is already in the laughter of a child, the beauty of a sunrise, the quiet comfort of prayer, and the unexplainable

112

peace that comes when we surrender our burdens.

Sometimes God's presence feels like a blazing light, guiding us clearly. At other times, it feels like silence or absence, and even when we cannot perceive him, he is still there. Our task is to cultivate an awareness of his presence, training our inner senses to notice his movement and trust that he is always nearby.

God in Our Suffering
One of the most difficult aspects of the human journey is suffering. Loss, illness, broken relationships, disappointments—these experiences can shake our faith and make us question everything we thought we knew about God's goodness. In these painful moments, many of us ask, *"Where is God?"*

The answer is not always what we expect, but scripture assures us that God is closest when we feel most alone. *"The Lord is close to the brokenhearted and saves those who are crushed in spirit"* (Psalm 34:18). This verse became very real to me when my father was diagnosed with cancer in 2012.

At the time, my life was already overflowing with responsibilities. I was raising three young children, running a business, and managing a household while trying to care for my father with my mom by his side as his health declined. I was overwhelmed, exhausted, and often felt torn between my roles. There were nights when I cried silently after putting the children to bed, wondering if I could carry the weight of it all. I prayed for healing, pleading with God for a miracle. But as my father's illness progressed, I realized that the miracle wasn't always the physical healing I had hoped for—it was the deepened faith, the strengthened resilience, and the precious moments of connection we shared.

I will never forget one night when my father looked at me with fear in his eyes because we were both afraid of him dying, and said in a gentle voice, *"God will hear our prayer."* Those words stayed with me. Even in his suffering, his faith was unwavering. He knew God was by his side. He showed me that grief and gratitude can exist side by side, and that God's presence is often most tangible in our darkest hours.

When we deepen our personal relationship with God, it allows us to feel His presence in whatever season we're experiencing.

A Spiritual Director or Companion can journey with us in exploring our relationship with God.

Reflection:
Recall a time of pain in your life. How did you experience God then? Were there moments of comfort, support, or unexpected strength that you now see as God's strength?

Role of a Spiritual Director
A spiritual director is a certified and trained Christian who accompanies another Christian as they cultivate, grow, and unravel how God and the Holy Spirit manifest in their daily life. It is a process with the person's actual experiences with God.

Reasons to Seek Spiritual Direction

- Hunger for something more than the world has to offer
- An awareness of something "Missing;" A search for wholeness

- A life transition-in a relationship, at work, at home, etc.
- A feeling of "Spiritual dryness"
- A feeling of being spiritually "stuck"
- A desire to place a spiritual "lens" on significant life decisions-<u>discernment</u>
- A desire for a deeper relationship with God

Issues/questions That May Come up in a Spiritual Direction Session

- Who is God for me, and where is God in my life
- What is, or isn't, going on between me and God
- What kind of relationship do I have with God, and God with me
- Who am I as I stand before God
- How am I living my life in relationship to God?
- How should I decide on an issue; what choices are before me?

As a certified and trained spiritual director and companion, I am dedicated to empowering people to embark on a meaningful journey of spiritual growth and personal transformation. My focus is on supporting people to deepen their faith, refresh their minds, and cultivate a genuine connection with God's Word. Through my companionship, people embrace authentic and fulfilling lives that honor God and inspire those around them. For more on Spiritual direction and companioning, please visit my website at:

www.tlifecoachinggrief.com

Closing Reflection & Prayer

Pause for a moment. Breathe deeply. Imagine God's presence beside you now. What is He whispering to your heart?

God of love and mercy, thank You for being with me in every season—in joy and in sorrow, in growth and in stillness. Help me to trust Your presence in my suffering, to walk in faith each day, to forgive myself as You have forgiven me, and to live out of the deep truth of Your love.

Thank You for the ways You speak, in silence, in scripture, and even in dreams. Give me discernment to recognize Your voice, and courage to follow where You lead.

Amen.

The Daily Practice of Faith

Faith isn't only for the stormy seasons. It is the steady, grounding presence in the ordinary and the extraordinary alike. In my own life, I have found that faith is cultivated in daily practices—simple but powerful rhythms that open my heart to God's voice.

One practice that has transformed me is the **Examen**, a prayer taught by St. Ignatius of Loyola. Each evening, I take time to review my day: Where did I feel God's presence? Where did I feel far away from Him? Where was I most alive, and where did I feel drained? This daily habit helps me recognize God's hand in the smallest details and to realign my heart when I wander.

How to Pray the Examen (Step-by-Step)

What it is:

The Examen is a brief, prayerful review of your day to notice God's presence, receive insight, and choose your next faithful step. Classic Ignatian practice; ~10–15 minutes; ideal at day's end (or midday reset).

Preparation (1 minute)

- Choose a quiet spot. Sit comfortably; feet grounded; slow a few breaths.

- Ask for help. "Holy Spirit, help me see my day as You see it—with honesty, mercy, and hope."

- (Optional) Keep a journal handy to jot a line or two after each step.

The Classic Five Steps (8–12 minutes)
1) Become Aware of God's Presence (1–2 min)

- Let your breath settle.

- Imagine God lovingly attentive to you right now.

- Simple prayer: *"Lord, here I am. Be with me as I look back."*

2) Give Thanks (1–2 min)

- Name 3–5 gifts from today—big or small: a smile, safe travel, a good meal, a moment of courage.

- Let gratitude soften your heart.

Prompt: *What am I most grateful for today — and why?*

3) Ask for Light (30 sec)

- Invite insight: *"Spirit of truth, show me my day clearly—without denial or harshness."*

4) Review the Day with God (4–6 min)

Gently "rewind" the day (morning → evening). Notice:

- Moments of consolation (movement toward God faith/hope/love; peace, courage, generosity).

- Moments of desolation (movement away or feeling distance from God; fear, apathy, resentment, isolation).

- What stirred your heart? What patterns reappeared? Where did you give/receive love?

Reflection Prompts:

- *When did I feel most alive, connected, or free today?*

- *When did I feel blocked, small, anxious, or reactive?*

- *What was I seeking in those moments? What might You have been offering, Lord?*

5) Respond: Mercy & Tomorrow's Grace (2–3 min)

- Ask forgiveness where needed; receive it. No self-beating, just truth and trust.

- Choose one concrete step for tomorrow (gentle and doable) and ask for grace to live it.

Prayer: *"God of mercy, thank You. Give me grace to (name your next step) tomorrow. Amen."*

Faith in daily life also shows up in the way we treat ourselves. For years, I believed that being strong meant never asking for help. But caregiving taught me that true strength is admitting when we need support. Faith invites us to trust not only God but also the community He places around us.

Reflection:
What is one small daily practice you can begin today to become more aware of God's presence in your life?

Growing into Your Purpose

Ultimately, grief and faith are both teachers. Grief teaches us about loss, impermanence, and the deep love we carry for those who have gone before us. Faith teaches us that even in loss, life continues—and with God, hope is never extinguished.

When we integrate grief and faith, we begin to see that our lives are not just about survival but about transformation. As I cared for my father and wrestled with my own pain, I found my calling as a life and grief coach. What was once a season of heaviness became the soil for my purpose: to walk alongside others in their own times of transition, loss, and self-discovery.

You, too, have a purpose that is unfolding. The dreams you carry, the faith you nurture, and the resilience you build through suffering are all part of the legacy you are creating. Living with God's presence doesn't remove the storms, but it gives you an anchor, so you are never swept away.

Reflection Prompts

Take a few moments to journal or reflect on these questions:

- Recall a season of loss or disappointment in your life. Where did you notice God's presence?

- What spiritual practices—prayer, journaling, meditation, Scripture reading—help you connect most deeply with God each day?

- Who has modeled faith and resilience for you in ways that inspire your own journey?

- What dream has God planted in your heart, and how might it guide your steps toward greater purpose?

- How can you begin to live more intentionally in God's love today?

Chapter 9: Living with Legacy and Purpose

"Your legacy is not just what you leave behind, but the love, lessons, and light you share along the way."

-Antoinette A. Enohmbi

The Call to Live with Intention

Every human heart longs for meaning. Deep down, we all want to know that our lives matter—that our presence in this world makes a difference beyond our own immediate needs and circumstances. This longing is not an accident. It is woven into us by God, who created us with purpose and invites us to live with intention.

For years, I believed that my worth was tied to my achievements. I thought if I could collect degrees, climb ladders, or prove myself in the eyes of others, then my life would mean something. Yet, no matter how many accomplishments I made, there was still emptiness inside, a quiet whisper reminding me: *There is more to life than this.*

That whisper was God's invitation. It called me to stop measuring success by society's standards and to begin asking: *What will my life stand for when I am no longer here? What seeds am I planting today that will bloom tomorrow for my children, my community, and the world?*

Living with legacy and purpose begins when we take these questions seriously. It is about shifting from survival to intentional living, from rushing through life to cultivating meaning in every step.

Building Your Legacy
The beautiful truth about legacy is that you don't need to wait until the end of your life to create it. In fact, your legacy is being written every single day in the small choices you make, the words you speak, and the love you extend.

Ask yourself:

- How do I want to be remembered by my family, my friends, and my community?

- What values do I want to embody so that others are inspired by my life?

- What do I want to give to the world that will outlast me?

Your legacy does not have to be something grand or public. It does not have to be a foundation with your name on it or a long list of accolades. Sometimes the most powerful legacy is the way you treated people with kindness, patience, and grace.

I often remind my clients that *purpose is not found in extraordinary moments alone, but in the way we choose to live the ordinary ones.* It is in how we love our children, how we forgive our neighbors, how we serve in our communities, and how we choose faith over fear each day.

Purpose: An Invitation to Flourish

Purpose is not something we create out of thin air—it is something we uncover. A gift from birth, long before we recognize it. Our role is to pause, listen, and respond.

Purpose became clear to me during the season of my father's illness and passing. At first, I resisted, felt inadequate, overwhelmed, and unsure why God would allow me to face such pain. Through prayer, spiritual direction, and reflection, I began to see that God was using my experiences to reveal my gift. He was shaping me to become a companion for others walking through life's storms.

Purpose is often born out of struggle. The very experiences we wish we could erase sometimes hold the keys to our greatest calling. Our pain can soften us, deepening our compassion. Our challenges can sharpen our vision, clarifying what really matters, and our losses can push us toward lives of greater meaning.

Living with purpose is not about doing more but about doing what matters most. It is about aligning your daily choices with your true calling, whether that means being a source of encouragement to your family, starting a new career, serving your community, or simply living with gratitude.

The Role of Faith in Legacy
Without faith, legacy can easily become achievement, recognition, or possessions, but with faith, legacy takes on an eternal

dimension. It is no longer just about what we leave *behind*, but about what we send *ahead*.

True legacy is not about perfection, but perseverance. It is about showing up day after day, trusting in yourself, and choosing to love even when life is difficult.

Faith invites us to think generationally. What if the way you respond to grief, to challenges, and to change becomes the model that your children and grandchildren carry into their own lives? What if your decision to lean into positivity instead of fear becomes the legacy that inspires someone else to keep going when they want to give up?

Your legacy is being shaped not only by what you accomplish but also by how you live, forgive, and love.

Reflection Prompt:
What values has your faith instilled in you that you hope to pass on to the next generation?

Living the Legacy Today

Too often, we think of legacy as something that will be read about at our funeral. But legacy is not simply a final chapter—it is every chapter. It is the way you treat the cashier at the grocery store, the patience you show when your child spills the milk, the compassion you extend to a grieving friend, and the courage you summon to chase a dream.

Living with legacy means living as if every action is a seed. Some seeds will grow quickly, others may take years to bloom, and some you may never see the fruit of in your lifetime. But every seed matters. Legacy multiplies in ways we cannot predict.

Living with legacy also requires us to think about **consistency**. It is not enough to do one generous act and call it a day. Legacy is built in the repetition of love, forgiveness, and service. It is formed when people know they can depend on your kindness, your integrity, and your faith.

Practical Ways to Live Your Legacy Now:

1. Write your values. Make a list of the five values you want your life to reflect.

2. Practice daily gratitude. Write down three things each day that you are thankful for.

3. Invest in people. Look for ways to mentor, encourage, or support someone in your circle.

4. Forgive quickly. Refuse to let grudges harden your heart.

5. Celebrate progress. Recognize the small victories in your journey as part of your legacy.

A Personal Word of Encouragement

When I think of legacy and purpose, I return again to my father's example. He lived simply, but he lived fully. His humility made him approachable. His generosity opened doors for others. His forgiveness created healing where bitterness could have taken root.

He taught me that legacy is not a grand monument. It is the gentle impact you make on others' lives. It is the smile that lightens someone's burden, the prayer whispered on behalf of another, the courage to love without expecting anything in return.

As I carry his memory, I am reminded that our lives preach sermons even when our lips are silent. What we do and how we love leaves an imprint. My father's life inspires me every day in my work as a life and grief coach and spiritual director. His example fuels my desire to help others live with meaning, hope, and a deep connection to God.

Closing Reflection

Take a moment to breathe deeply. Place your hand over your heart and imagine the kind of legacy you hope to leave. See your children, grandchildren, friends, or community looking back at your life. What will they remember most?

Reflection Questions:

1. What is one word you would like others to use to describe you after you are gone?

2. What seeds of love, generosity, or faith are you planting today?

3. How might you invite God into the process of shaping your legacy?

Chapter 10: Conclusion to Transformative Life Coaching

"Every ending is a doorway to a new beginning, and every beginning is an invitation to live with greater purpose."

-Antoinette A. Enohmbi

The Journey of Coaching Through Time

When many people hear the term *life coaching*, they imagine it to be a modern innovation, something born out of the latest self-help trends. In truth, coaching, though it may not have always carried this exact name, has been woven into the fabric of human history for centuries.

If we look back to ancient Greece, we'll find that Socrates and his student Plato engaged in dialogues that resemble what we now call coaching conversations. These dialogues were not lectures but intentional conversations—filled with questions, challenges, reflection, and exploration. They were designed not to provide all the answers, but to help the student discover truth, meaning, and wisdom within themselves. This is the very heartbeat of coaching today: creating space where self-discovery can happen.

In more recent times, modern coaching as we know it was shaped significantly by the world of sports. Think of the baseball coach shouting encouragement from the sidelines, or the basketball coach who sees potential in a player that others might overlook. These coaches inspire confidence, sharpen skills, and push people beyond what they thought possible. The coaching mindset migrated beyond athletics into business, leadership, education, and eventually into the realm of personal and spiritual growth.

Over the past few decades, *whole-life coaching* has gained momentum. Unlike traditional executive coaching, which focuses mainly on productivity or career development, whole-life coaching acknowledges the interconnectedness of personal, professional, emotional, and spiritual well-being. More organizations are recognizing that when employees are holistically healthy, mentally, physically, emotionally, and spiritually, they perform better, collaborate more effectively, and contribute to a healthier work culture.

For leaders, incorporating coaching into the workplace is a profound way of supporting their teams. It means not only mentoring someone to reach their career goals but also recognizing the whole human being in front of them. When we nurture balance and fulfillment in people's lives, the ripple effects spread far beyond the office walls.

The Search for the Right Coach
If you've read this far, it is likely because you are curious about what coaching could mean for your life. You may already know that choosing a life coach is no simple task. Unlike some professions, life coaching is still largely unregulated. While this gives flexibility and room for creativity, it also means that anyone can call themselves a coach, set a rate, and start working with clients.

This lack of regulation can make the search confusing. You may wonder: *How do I know if this person is qualified? How do I know if they can truly help me?* These are important questions. While there isn't one universal pathway or certification that defines a life coach, there are many credible training institutions and professional bodies working diligently to raise standards in the field.

If you are considering working with a coach, I encourage you to do your research. Ask about their training, their approach, and their areas of specialty. A strong coach does not present themselves as someone who has all the answers. Instead, they serve as a guide, a mirror, and a companion who supports you and discovers the wisdom and strength already present within you.

If you are considering becoming a spiritual director, there are credible faith-based training formation institutions that provide thorough education, mentorship, and accountability such as the World On Fire Spiritual Formation program (WOF) and Peacock Soul Care formation (PSC)

Attaining Your Goals Through Coaching
One of the most practical benefits of coaching is its ability to help you clarify and pursue your goals. A transformative life coach helps you look at where you are now and then guides you to where you long to be. Together, we explore the gap between your present reality and your desired future, breaking it down into

steps that are both manageable and meaningful.

Here are some common goals that coaching can support:

- Career Shifts: Exploring new paths, transitioning to a role that aligns with your values, or developing the courage to step into leadership.

- Entrepreneurship: Starting a new business or revitalizing an existing one, supported by strategy and mindset coaching.

- Relationships: Navigating challenges, deepening intimacy, or learning healthier communication patterns.

- Health & Wellness: Committing to exercise, healthier nutrition, or meaningful rest.

- Personal Habits: Breaking free from patterns that no longer serve you— whether it's smoking, procrastination, or negative self-talk.

- Financial Freedom: Learning to manage money wisely, build wealth, or shift from scarcity thinking to an abundance mindset.

- Confidence and Self-Worth: Building a strong sense of self that empowers you to pursue your dreams without apology.

When I began my journey, I thought success meant collecting degrees and checking boxes on society's list of accomplishments. I poured myself into academics, careers, and even into my responsibilities as a caregiver and a mother. But eventually, I learned that true success isn't found in external validation—it comes from aligning your life with your inner values and God's guidance.

A coach provides support, accountability, and perspective to help you prioritize your goals. If you're carrying a long list of dreams, coaching helps you discern which steps to take now and which to save for later. This process protects you from overwhelming and allows you to move forward with clarity and purpose.

Reinventing Your Life

Life is a journey of seasons, and each season invites us to reinvent ourselves. The start of a new year often stirs hope and optimism. We write resolutions: get healthier, grow spiritually, repair relationships, or achieve financial freedom. But research shows that over 80% of people abandon their New Year's resolutions by the end of January. Why? Because intentions without action remain dreams.

That old proverb comes to mind again: *"If wishes were horses, beggars would ride."* Wishing is easy, but living in a new reality requires courage, discipline, and support. Real reinvention does not happen in a single grand gesture. It happens in small, consistent choices—choosing water instead of soda, taking a walk instead of staying glued to the screen, reaching out instead of withdrawing, saying a prayer instead of worrying.

I've learned to reinvent myself many times. As each year begins, I reflect on what God is inviting me into for the next chapter. In the early days of my career, I believed success meant accumulating degrees, certificates, and achievements. Later, motherhood reshaped that vision. Then, my father's illness and passing deepened my understanding of strength, faith, and compassion. Each reinvention has required me to pause, listen to God's whisper, and align my choices with who I am becoming.

Reinvention is not about discarding who you are. It is about uncovering the essence of who God created you to be and allowing that truth to shine more fully in your life.

Choosing Legacy and Purpose
At the heart of transformative life coaching is the belief that you were created for a purpose. That purpose is not static; it grows and evolves with you. Your dreams, your griefs, your love, your faith, all these experiences shape your legacy. Legacy is not only about what you leave behind when your life is over. It is about how you live today. It is about the lives you touch, the kindness you show, the forgiveness you extend, and the love you share.

Your legacy will be written in how you love and serve others. Purpose is not only about big accomplishments but about the daily choices
139

you make. Do you offer kindness when it is inconvenient? Do you extend grace when it is not deserved?

When we live with purpose, we naturally create a legacy that outlives us. Our children, friends, and communities will remember not the titles we held, but the love we shared.

Reflection Questions:
- What kind of legacy do I want to leave behind?

- How do my daily choices reflect my deeper purpose?

- In what ways can I honor the people who shaped me by living out the best of what they taught me?

From Reading to Living
As we conclude this book, I want to invite you into a gentle but powerful challenge: do not let these words remain on the page. Transformation begins when you apply what you have read to your life. Reading about dreams, love, faith, and grief can inspire you,

but it is only when you integrate these insights into your daily actions that real change occurs.

Here are some guiding steps to move from reading to living:

1. Reflect – Set aside time to revisit the parts of this book that touched you most. What spoke to your heart? What patterns do you notice in your own life story?

2. Write – Keep a journal where you record your thoughts, dreams, prayers, and reflections. Writing creates clarity and helps track your growth.

3. Act – Choose one small step you can take this week toward a healthier, more purposeful life. It may be reaching out to a friend, setting a new boundary, or creating a daily gratitude practice.

4. Pray and Discern – Invite God into the process. Ask Him to guide your steps and open your heart to His whispers.

5. Connect – Transformation rarely happens in isolation. Share your

journey with a trusted friend, community, or spiritual director who can walk with you and reflect your growth back to you.

6. Celebrate – Acknowledge your progress, no matter how small. Every step forward is evidence of courage, faith, and growth.

Final Encouragement

As you move forward, remember this truth: you are not broken, you are becoming. Every loss, every challenge, every dream, and every act of love is part of your unique journey toward wholeness. The path of transformative life coaching is not about fixing who you are; it is about uncovering the beauty, strength, purpose, and gifts that were present in you at birth.

My hope is that this book has inspired you to begin or to continue your journey of transformation. Whether you are stepping into a new season of life, seeking healing from grief, or longing to live with deeper purpose, know that you are not alone. Help is within reach.

As your coach and companion, I am here to support you. I will walk with you as you discover the fullness of who you are meant to be. I will help you ask the questions that bring clarity, embrace the practices that bring peace, and take the steps that lead to transformation.

The next chapter of your life is waiting. The canvas is blank. The colors are in your hands. Together, let us paint a masterpiece.

Reflection Exercise – Stepping into Your Next Chapter
- Write down three lessons from your own life journey that you want to carry forward.

- Name one dream you've been postponing that you're ready to pursue.

- Reflect on how God's love and presence might strengthen you as you step into this next season.

- Ask yourself: *If I believed I already had everything I needed, what would I begin to explore?*

Resources for Your Ongoing Journey

"The tools we choose shape the path we walk."

Why Resources Matter on the Transformative Journey

Transformation is not a one-time event; it is a continuous unfolding of who we are becoming. Just as a seed requires soil, water, and sunlight to grow, our journeys of life coaching, grief work, and spiritual growth require nourishment. Resources-books, courses, tools, communities, and practices serve as companions on the path. They provide guidance, fresh perspectives, encouragement, and wisdom when our own clarity wavers.

As a Certified Life Coach and Spiritual Director, I have drawn from many sources: scripture, spiritual mentors, personal experiences of joy and grief, and practical tools developed by leaders in psychology, coaching, and spirituality. The following resources are not a rigid curriculum but a living toolkit. They are meant to be used prayerfully and intentionally, adapted to your unique needs and season of life.

Books to Inspire and Equip You

Books are windows into wisdom—voices that travel across time and space to meet us where we are. Each of the books below has shaped my own journey and continues to serve as a well I return to for guidance and encouragement.

1. *The One Minute Manager* by Ken Blanchard & Spencer Johnson; A timeless classic on leadership and coaching, this book demonstrates how small, intentional actions like one-minute goals, praises, and redirects can create meaningful change. Though written for leaders in business, its lessons apply to anyone desiring to encourage growth in themselves or others.
2. *The Big Leap* by Gay Hendricks

A powerful resource for anyone who feels stuck at the edge of their growth. Hendricks introduces the concept of the "upper limit problem"—the subconscious barriers that keep us from living into our highest potential—and guides readers to expand beyond fear into abundance.

3. *The Four Agreements* by Don Miguel Ruiz

   A life-giving invitation to live with freedom and authenticity. Ruiz's four principles—be impeccable with your word, don't take anything personally, don't make assumptions, and always do your best—offer practical wisdom for daily living.

4. *Radical Acceptance* by Tara Brach

   A compassionate guide for anyone struggling with self-criticism, shame, or a sense of unworthiness. This book integrates mindfulness and spiritual wisdom to help us embrace ourselves as we are, even in our brokenness.

5. *A Friendship Like No Other* by William Barry

   This book deeply influenced my own journey with God. Barry presents prayer not as a ritual to be perfected but as a friendship to be nurtured. It reminded me that God desires closeness with us, not performance.

6. *God and You: Prayer as a Personal Relationship* by William Barry

   Another profound work by Barry, this book reinforces the truth that there is no single "right" way to pray. It encourages us to speak to God honestly, as we would with a trusted friend, and to listen for His presence in return.

Together, these books create a rich library of insight, encouragement, and practical tools for both personal growth and professional development.

Courses and Certifications for Coaches and Seekers

For those who feel called to go deeper, whether to become a life or grief coach, or to embark on a spiritual formation journey, some programs and trainings provide structure, accountability, and wisdom.

1. International Coach Federation (ICF) Certification

   The ICF is the leading global body for professional coaching. Their programs provide credibility, mentorship, and a strong framework of *Core Competencies* that help coaches create meaningful, transformative experiences for clients.

2. International Association of Professional Recovery Coaches (IAPRC)

   This program offers dynamic training that provides coaches with effective system which combines proven protocols of professional coaching and recovery. The depth and quality of course materials come from clinical research.

3. The Institute of Professional Grief Coaching (IOPGC)

   This program provides coaches with the knowledge, skills, resources and confidence to guide clients through transformative journey of managing painful emotions of grief, reclaiming their sense of purpose, and moving forward in life with meaning

4. Institute for Professional Excellence in Coaching (iPEC)

   iPEC provides a comprehensive coaching certification rooted in core competencies and tools like the *Energy Leadership Index*, which helps clients understand how their energy and mindset impact every area of their lives.

5. Mind valley Coaching Certification Program

   This program blends personal development with coaching techniques, including emotional intelligence, mindset transformation, and spiritual growth.

6. World of Fire (WOF) Spiritual Formation Program

   A Christ-centered program designed to help individuals deepen their relationship with God and become trained spiritual directors. It focuses on discernment, prayer practices, and integrating faith into every area of life.

7. Peacock Soul Care Spiritual Formation (PCS) Program

   This program is designed to trained Spiritual Director. It equips participants to walk alongside others with compassion, while nurturing their own inner life and spiritual well-being.

These programs provide different pathways for those who feel called to guide others or grow spiritually. Some focus more on coaching and personal development, while others emphasize spiritual direction and companionship. Together, they offer a broad foundation for anyone seeking to become a source of light and support in their community.

Coaching Tools and Practices

Beyond books and formal programs, coaches and individuals benefit from practical tools that can be integrated into everyday life. These tools are simple yet profound ways to foster clarity, action, and transformation.

1. Neuro-Linguistic Programming (NLP) Techniques

   NLP offers tools such as anchoring, reframing, and visualization to help shift unhelpful thought patterns and create new, empowering perspectives.

2. The Wheel of Life

   A visual tool that allows you to evaluate different areas of your life—such as health, relationships, career, finances, and spirituality—and identify where you feel balanced and where you long for growth.

3. Visualization Practices

   Guided imagery helps clients see and feel their desired future, engaging both mind and heart in the process of transformation.

4. The GROW Model *(Goal, Reality, Options, Will)*

   A practical coaching framework that helps clarify goals, understand current realities, brainstorm possibilities, and commit to actionable steps.

5. Journaling Prompts

   Reflective writing can unlock insights that stay hidden in daily life. Prompts such as:

   o *What does my ideal life look like?*

   o *What limiting beliefs are holding me back?*

   o *How would my life change if I released fear or self-doubt?*

6. The Miracle Question

A powerful tool from Solution-Focused Brief Therapy that invites clients to imagine a sudden breakthrough. This question opens the heart to possibility and helps clarify what truly matters.

7. StrengthsFinder Assessment

Identifying your top strengths provides a foundation for growth. Rather than fixing weaknesses, this tool encourages clients to maximize their unique gifts.

8. Mindfulness and Spiritual Practices

Practices such as meditation, deep breathing, prayer, or silent reflection help us stay present, grounded, and open to God's gentle guidance.

Podcasts and Audio Resources

Sometimes, transformation happens not in a structured session but while driving to work, washing dishes, or taking a walk. Podcasts and audio resources allow us to receive wisdom in the flow of daily life. Here are a few that I recommend:

1. The Life Coach School Podcast by *Brooke Castillo* – Practical coaching tools and mindset shifts.

2. The Mel Robbins Podcast – Motivational insights and strategies for growth.

3. The Mindful Coach Podcast – Guidance on integrating mindfulness into the coaching journey and into daily life.

Communities of Support
Transformation is not meant to be walked alone. We thrive in the presence of others who encourage, challenge, and remind us of who we are becoming. Joining communities provides connection, accountability, and inspiration.

1. International Coach Federation (ICF) Chapters – Connect with coaches worldwide, attend conferences, and learn from a global community.

2. The Transformational Coaching Community (Facebook) – A space to share stories, tools, and encouragement with like-minded people.

3. LinkedIn Coaching Groups – Online communities where professionals share insights, resources, and opportunities.

Discovering Your Behavioral Style
Self-awareness is the foundation of transformation. The following framework, often called a *behavioral style matrix*, helps you reflect on your tendencies in relationships and decision-making. There is no right or wrong column—simply different ways of being.

156

Table: Finding Your Behavioral Style

Column A	Column B	Column C	Column D
Avoids risks	Embraces risks	Relaxed and warm	Formal and proper
Slow to decide	Quick to decide	Opinion-oriented	Fact-oriented
Indirect	Direct	Open	Reserved
Easygoing	Impatient	Shares feelings	Keeps feelings in
Relationship focus	Task focus	Intuitive	Analytical

Use this table as a mirror, not a judgment. Which column do you see yourself in most often? How does your natural style help you? In what ways might it limit you?

Final Encouragement

Resources are gifts, but they are not the journey itself. Books, courses, tools, and communities can point us in the right direction, but transformation happens when we show up, engage with courage, and allow God to move in our lives.

I encourage you to explore these resources with an open heart. Let them challenge you, comfort you, and expand your vision of what is possible. Use them to deepen your relationship with yourself, with others, and with God.

Remember: **you are not alone.** You have access to a world of wisdom and companionship—mentors, coaches, spiritual directors, communities, and resources that will walk with you. Allow these tools to serve as steppingstones as you continue your journey from grief to gratitude, from confusion to clarity, from surviving to thriving.

The journey is lifelong, but every step you take matters. Let these resources support you as you keep painting the masterpiece of your life. - Antoinette A. Enohmbi

Contact Me:
If these words have spoken to you and you are ready to begin your journey of transformation; I invite you to reach out. My coaching practice is a safe and supportive space where your dreams, struggles, and faith are honored.

Transformative Life Coaching, LLC

Antoinette (Anti) Abe Okala Enohmbi – Certified Life & Grief Coach, Spiritual Director

Phone: 301-404-4261
Website: www.tlifecoachinggrief.com
Email: antoinette@tlifecoachinggrief.com